ISLAND

ISLAND

Our Alaskan dream and reality

Joy Orth

ALASKA NORTHWEST PUBLISHING COMPANY
Edmonds, Washington

Library of Congress Cataloging-in-Publication Data

Orth, Joy, 1925-
Our Alaskan island.

Bibliography: p.
1. Sergief Island (Alaska) — Social life and customs.
2. Country life — Alaska — Sergief Island. 3. Orth, Joy, 1925- . 4. Sergief Island (Alaska) — Biography.
I. Title.
F912.S27077 1987 979.8'2 87-1308
ISBN 0-88240-321-4CIP

Cover design by Shawn Lewis
Photos by Joy Orth and Jeff Orth
Printed in U.S.A.

Island in the Stikine. Sergief Island sits in the stream of one of North America's last great free rivers — it, too, now threatened by the proponents of progress.

This book is written with the hope that the lives and workings on one small island might grow to be meaningful to some who look for another way to live; that what we've learned here might be of use to others; that in the stream of time and circumstance it might be an island of certitude and peace.

CONTENTS

The Stikine River winds through its lower basin.

I
WHERE, OH WHERE?

The cries of the gulls echo through the cabin in the early morning chill, becoming louder as I come down the ladder from the loft. On reaching the window I can see the white clouds of their bodies as they swirl over the Stikine River waters. The tide is coming in, bringing with it the first run of hooligan, silvery members of the candlefish family that come by the million each year to spawn in the river. Now the gulls cry as they dive in a frenzy of anticipation for their catch. A pair of bald eagles patrols the beach in a clumsy, heavy-footed manner, belying their graceful majesty in the air.

The sun has just cleared the green mountains of the eastern mainland, its bright rays fracturing the rippled surface of the water into millions of pieces of shining light. Here and there the round head of a seal surfaces; it, too, has come to join in the feast. It's a good day to be alive in Southeast Alaska. Time to be up and about.

True, it isn't a day strictly typical of our climate of heavy rainfall, but there are enough days like this to make one glad to be here and the remainder easy to overlook.

My family and I haven't always lived on an island. Most of our lives have been spent in western Washington. When we moved to our island home in Alaska five years ago, it was after a long process of decision-making and shopping for just the right place. We came, my husband, Lloyd; sons, Lee and Jeff; daughter, Sethnie; and I; along with our nephew, Neal; his wife, Deveril; and baby, Jacob; from a conventional middle-class way of life, each bringing ideas of how things were going to be, living in the "wilderness." Most of those ideas called for considerable revision.

Home is now one hundred and fourteen acres of land on Sergief Island, located in a designated wilderness area. By the time we closed the deal late in 1979, and were actually moving, we'd been looking long enough to know what an extraordinary happening this was.

We first started thinking of making a radical change in our way of life after a summer trip to British Columbia in 1967. We had suffered a great loss to our family the year before that caused us to examine ourselves and our lives and begin to think that perhaps a life closer to nature, not so geared to material possessions, would be a thing to be desired.

British Columbia is magnificent country. We saw, that summer and subsequent years, lands that took our breath away: mountains and rivers of such beauty we each felt a catch in our hearts. We explored the areas around the Bulkley and Kispiox rivers, and later the Chilko River area, west of Williams Lake. Although they were ever to be remembered, we had no way, at that time, to take possession of any of the available lands.

There were, then, still Canadian land programs open to non-residents of Canada. This has changed, but even then, available parcels were hard to locate and were strictly regulated as to use.

Things went on in a similar vein over the next few years. We were busy. We sold our home and bought another piece of land in Washington state. It too was beautiful and comfortable, but it wasn't wilderness. Lloyd became more engrossed in his business of land clearing and we became ever more deeply engaged in work for our church. The years sped, but the idea of a move to a remote area was never extinguished from our minds.

On one trip to British Columbia we'd just missed a large parcel of land on the upper Kispiox River that was in the process of changing hands. It had been, at one time, a hunting camp, and had cabins built on a bluff overlooking the river and a beautiful meadow. The Hazelton Mountains rose in the foreground, towering spruce to the back; I held it in my heart and thought it to be the most beautiful place I'd ever seen — until I saw Sergief Island.

In 1978 we made our first trip to Southeast Alaska. In the autumn of that year we set out, this time pulling a fifth-wheel trailer that made our travels considerably more comfortable. We went up, again, through British Columbia, following the Skeena River basin to Prince Rupert; flew over some land for sale on Porcher Island; then backtracked to Terrace, where we turned onto the newly completed Cassiar Highway. The Cassiar is a 400-mile stretch of wilderness road, rugged by anybody's standards. A few miles before coming to Dease Lake we crossed the Stikine River for the first time. Little did I know how important the crossing of that river would become in my life.

At Watson Lake we joined the Alaska Highway and continued through Yukon Territory to Whitehorse and on to Haines Junction, where we turned south and finally entered ALASKA. To me it was thrilling, fulfilling a dream, and if we didn't find the place we were looking for in Haines (which we didn't), the visit did whet our appetite for Alaska. We saw hundreds of eagles gathered to feast along the waterways of Haines, some bears along the highways, and salmon by the thousand in many of the creeks. We went home with renewed determination to find our spot in the wilderness.

I had written to the Office of Land Management in Juneau. At that time the disposal of all public lands was frozen until the settlement of the Native Land Claims Act, so we pretty much gave up on that way of acquiring land. I then wrote to every real estate agency in Southeast Alaska that I could get a lead on, told them what we were looking for, and began watching the mailbox.

We wanted a fair-size piece of acreage, timbered, with some tillable soil, on the water, and in Southeast, which has a fairly moderate climate, similar to what we were used to in western Washington. I was especially interested in finding land in the Stikine River basin, since I'd read in *The MILEPOST®* that the area had once produced hay and grain for the pack animals used in gold-rush days. My reasoning was that if the soil and climate were capable of growing what was needed for those animals, it would surely be able to produce the vegetable needs of a family or group of families. After living here these past years I still don't know how they got their hay up, but I'm giving it continuing thought.

When I went out to meet the mailman one day in the early spring of 1979, I received a letter from Mary Buness, of the Buness Realty in Wrangell, with a lot of enthusiasm. Mary wrote that she was handling a 114-acre piece of land on Sergief Island in the Stikine River estuary. It was within our price range, so I got on the phone. Mary described the land to me. It had timber, two springs, a few old buildings and land that could grow anything the climate would permit. Mary said the island was on the flyway of many kinds of waterfowl, and in spring the lower island was ablaze with millions of wildflowers. I couldn't wait to see it.

When my husband and our nephew, Neal, flew up in April, I saw them off with a bit of envy. They had some leads on other pieces of land to look at, but when they stepped onto Sergief Island, they both said later, they felt they'd come to thc end of a long search. They'd found it.

Then began a flurry of negotiations; the place wasn't all that easy to buy. Although the owners had had it listed for sale for some time, they seemed to have second thoughts when the actual offer came. Large pieces of privately owned land are scarce articles in Southeast Alaska, and pieces where a going homestead can be worked are scarcer still. The land, except for a small percentage owned by the State of Alaska, the Native tribes, and the various small townships dotting the area, is all part of the federally owned and managed Tongass National Forest. We wanted the piece on the Stikine badly, and when the deal finally closed we felt that was the way it was meant to be.

We still had land in Washington to sell. We had horses to sell or find boarding places for. Most of all, we had to figure out the best way to transport tools, furniture, building materials, boats and personal items to Wrangell. We needed to decide whether to ship our belongings commercially or transport them ourselves — by ferry from Seattle, or overland to Prince Rupert and the remaining way by ferry.

We opted to buy a large van, build a flatbed trailer, load the pickup, and drive to Prince Rupert, there to finish the way to Wrangell by water. Even with all that carrying ability it still took three round trips to complete the move. And then, of course, we still were not on Sergief Island, but only in Wrangell. For the final water lap we built a barge, an ungainly thing that, nevertheless, did the job.

The men of the family made the first trip in October of '79, staying a few days on the island, storing the belongings they'd taken with them in Wrangell, finishing the construction of the barge, and getting the general feel of the land.

When they started back home, Lee and Neal stayed behind on Sergief to cut wood and, as much as they were able, make the place ready for our winter occupation.

Sethnie, Deveril, and I were in Washington, preparing to go up on the next trip.

All these things weren't accomplished without a pang on my part — and probably on the parts of the others. Nobody let on.

I was going, sight unseen, to a way of life unfamiliar to me. We weren't just moving to Alaska; we were moving to a life style where subsistence with as little coming in from outside as possible would be the aim. I was leaving behind many people I loved — an aged mother and mother-in-law, two grown children and their families, many other relatives and friends. Sometimes I questioned the wisdom of the whole project, but I thought there were reasons for the move.

In the first place, I never expected to live on the island alone. Looking back over the years I've been here, I can see that I operated on an abundance of optimistic fantasy. In my mind I saw a bustling little community of cooperative people working together to build cottage industries and community buildings, with a relationship of freedom that would draw others to them.

My role, as I saw it, would be grandmother to the babies, friend and counselor to the young, and help to all, part of a vanguard to prepare the way for those who would come later.

I envisioned tea parties for the youngsters who would surely visit me in the afternoons, small candle-lit dinner parties for their parents, picnics on the beach, potlucks and barbecues. It was quite a picture, and if I can now smile at myself it is still not without a tug of the heart at the hopes of mice — and women.

So, after all the preparations, the trundling back and forth, all the problems we encountered trailering our boat through severe weather in British Columbia, when, finally, the ferry, *Taku*, drew in sight of the lights of Wrangell on that bitterly cold night in December of 1979, I felt a thrill of fear and sadness. My bridges were burned, but if I could have, I might, right then, have turned around and retraced my way. Possibly women down through the ages, making moves far greater and more conclusive than mine, have felt that chill as they prepared to meet the unknown.

Our entry into Wrangell wasn't exactly a notable occasion. It was after midnight; Southeast Alaska was suffering its first crackdown of winter, with temperatures around zero and bone-chilling winds sweeping down from the Arctic. We left the ice-encrusted decks of the *Taku* for the ice-encrusted ramp and road of the ferry terminal. The only really warm things seemed to be the faces of Lee and Neal as they met us after getting off Sergief Island just in time to beat the last storm.

The boys had spent their first nights in town on Neal's boat, but, finding it hard to keep warm, they moved headquarters into the unused laundromat building we'd rented to store our furniture. Feeling unable, or unwilling, to afford motel rates for so many, we moved in too. The two kerosene heaters and a borrowed electric heater took the chill off, barely, but the hide-a-bed looked inviting and to those on the floor the warmth radiating from the body of our big black Labrador, Smeller, was welcome.

If we'd been more knowledgeable about Stikine country we'd have known that to make a move such as we proposed in the latter part of December was very nearly impossible.

Sergief Island is about eight miles from Wrangell, subject to the saltwater tides and the fresh waters of the Stikine. To reach it you must negotiate three distinct weather patterns, as well as the tides.

As the river races toward its mouth it divides and subdivides, forming numerous channels and islands in the process. As it passes Sergief Island it spreads itself into so many rivulets that a channel is sometimes hard to find, so crossings are usually made when the tides have pushed enough salt water over the flats to make crossing easy. Even then, many an unwary boater finds himself stranded on a bar. He must either get out and push, if his boat is small enough, or wait for the next tide to come in and rescue him from his dilemma.

Coming from Wrangell, your first concern is the condition of the water in front of Wrangell Island, where it is primarily influenced by the tide and a possible south or west wind. If you see heavy swells or lots of white water, you stay in Wrangell. If all looks well, you proceed along the island to the end where the airport is poised on the tip. The channel from there to the mainland is referred to locally as the "back channel." It's there that you're most apt to run into seas that make you wish you'd stayed home. Winds can blow down that channel with great force, and often change dramatically in a matter of minutes. If these two microclimates have been to your liking, you're still not home free. Often, especially in fall and early spring, as you reach the influence of the winds funneling down from the northeast out of the Stikine basin you find yourself caught in an icy blast of fifty miles per hour or more. It can be a sobering experience, and several times I've found myself calculating whether or not I could make it to shore if the boat should be swamped. When we scuttle into our little cove it is often with a prayer of thanksgiving.

We knew none of these things in December 1979, but we did know that we weren't going to make it when we tried an exploratory run and found a thickening skin of ice on the water over the flats a couple of miles from the island. Local folks told us that the river sometimes opens again during the winter, so we settled down to await the end of the cold snap.

Wrangell is a very small town — around two thousand people — and our entry did not go unobserved. Most folks welcomed us heartily with words of wisdom, but a few looked at our little project with amusement or dislike, apparently thinking they'd just as soon we'd go back to wherever we'd come from. For one thing, the site on Sergief Island had been used for quite a few years as a hunting camp or general stopover for many local river runners. To see strangers, Cheechakos at that, moving onto their river didn't set too well with some. We hope, and believe, that over the years we've become friends.

Others, learning of our sorry state in the frigid laundromat, went out of their way to help us. We'd had no intention of camping there more than a night or two, but the days dragged on. Lieutenant and Mrs. Jerry Akin of the Salvation Army made repeated trips to pick us up for midweek meetings, a Christmas party, and even dinner at their home. We received friendship and hospitality from various members of the Seventh Day Adventist Church. Dick Stokes, a local tribal chief, loaned us his electric heater and helped in any way he could. John Ellis offered friendship and invaluable advice; probably no one knows the river better than he. (In our first years on the river, when he was salvaging logs or hauling freight for logging or fishing camps up the Canadian part of the river, it was consoling to know that John would probably soon be by with his big wave and help, if needed.) Carolee Thruston always had a hot cup of herb tea handy at her Better Way

Health Food Store, along with a smile. Mary Buness brought us Christmas cookies, and during the first week of January came by to say there was a house on Church Street that we could rent for the winter — if we were interested. If we were interested! We were ecstatic, and the three rooms with a bathroom and hot water seemed like a choice suite at the Hilton.

We began to catch our breath and settle down. I enrolled Jeff and Sethnie in Alaska Centralized Correspondence Study, an option to anyone in Alaska, because we still expected to get to the island at any time. Neal decided to go back to Washington until spring, and Lloyd took the van in February to make the last trip for our possessions. Jeff, sixteen then, and Sethnie, eleven, with Lee and me along with the two dogs, Smeller and Taffy, were left in Wrangell for a few months to learn our way around. It was a good experience, a healing time for my frazzled nerves. I like Wrangell; I like its people. But my heart belongs on Sergief Island.

I first set foot on it on March 17, 1980. The ice was well out of the river but there were still patches of snow on the ground. As I climbed up the bank from the beach and looked at the tiny, grubby cabin that would soon be home, it didn't seem like such a monstrous undertaking, after all. I saw the beautiful varicolored rocks along the beach and in back of the cabin and the windblown spruce coming, in places, down to the water. There was even a petite white weasel to greet us. I took a deep breath of the oh-so-pure air and gave thanks that I'd be privileged to live here; I prayed it would be for the good of the young people. I felt that after all the looking, conjecture, and everything that had gone into our getting here, I was finally where I was intended to be. The island would become home.

The new combination chicken house/greenhouse/root cellar goes up — and up!

II

A ROOF OVERHEAD, WATER AND HEAT

When we started thinking of remote living I had various visions of living accommodations, depending upon the particular place we were looking at. My imagination ran the gamut of possible homes, from beautifully crafted lodge-type log dwellings to earth-sheltered models or energy-efficient solar types, to remodeling jobs on easily renovated out-of-use canneries. I considered them all — and I've got the books to prove it. I was intimate with all the success stories in *Mother Earth* magazine; if they could do it, we could too.

Our ideas for building and remodeling were based on experience. Twice, in our married years, we'd undertaken major remodelings with add-ons. Once we took a tiny foundationless cottage and built it into what I considered a magnificent house of 3,300 square feet, complete with a two-story rock wall with a fireplace that took five-foot logs. When Lloyd was off earning the money that financed the project, a lot of the details and legwork fell to our son, Doug, and me. We hired help as we could afford it, so the total job took awhile. Doug and I even built a brick wall dividing kitchen and dining room with a support for a Franklin fireplace. We built it from the footings up to the second floor ceiling. If you looked close you could see that it wasn't always perfectly straight — Doug was fourteen and I wasn't a bricklayer — but it had a fine rustic look and we were proud of it. The folks who eventually bought the place liked it too.

When we moved farther out into the country to a larger piece of land, again we started with a house that had been badly neglected — not lived in for years — and made it into a home, adding a large rec room, bedroom and bath.

We thought we knew a lot about making the best of what

we had, so when we looked for remote land we hoped there would be usable buildings. I especially hoped we'd find an abandoned cannery or logging camp for sale. We got a lead on two of these: one on the Canadian coast, one in Alaska. They turned out to be far beyond our financial capabilities.

Acreage for sale, with or without buildings, is scarce in Alaska, so when it turned out there were a few old buildings on Sergief Island, everybody rejoiced. They weren't anything to get too excited about but they beat camping in the rain.

When we were completely moved onto the island in June of 1980, none of my previous experience had prepared me to deal with what I found. The cabin was a small frame building, 28 feet by 20 feet, with one partition and a falling-down back porch. It was weather-tight but the windows were small; the whole of everything was covered by a quarter inch of the dust that blows down from the upper river bars and filters down on the islands for miles around. (This dust does not arrive too often or for too long, or living here would be extremely unpleasant.) There were four bunks built along one wall and another double-sized bunk along another wall. A big barrel stove took up much of the main room; the water arrived on a sometimes basis through a plastic pipe on top of the ground. It was a depressing prospect, but when things got heavy in the cabin I had only to walk along the beach, or visit the garden area that we were tilling, to feel rejuvenated.

The weather cooperated with us splendidly that June; the water was gloriously brilliant from all the sunshine on it; the soil warmed rapidly. As I sifted the soft loam through my fingers I was happy to be on Sergief.

At one time this piece of the island had been a dairy farm where the animals were kept during the warm part of the year. The cows were barged over in the spring, pastured all summer, and barged back to Wrangell about Labor Day. During all those months the milk was taken each day, weather permitting, to Wrangell and delivered to homes and stores. My admiration for the sturdy, ambitious pioneers has grown as I've made the trips myself. To think of making them every day, rain or shine, boggles my mind. There's still a street in Wrangell called Cow Alley, commemorating the past presence of all those cows.

It seems that in the early decades of this century homesteaders, people trying to build a life, were on many of the islands of Southeast Alaska. Fox farms were prevalent; many kinds of berry and truck garden crops were attempted. The remnants of buildings and fences attest to the fact that few of them were successful. Perhaps when the original homesteaders died their children had little interest in staying. The homesteaders' efforts have gone back to nature, to be covered and obliterated by the salmonberry, thimbleberry and Indian celery. It's saddening, in a way, and I hope to one day find and examine many of these sites, learning what I can about each one and the people who labored there.

Just beyond us to the north is Farm Island, where burros and mules were pastured and cared for during gold-rush days. Some parcels of privately owned land on the island have great gardening soil. There are several cabins, but they're used only occasionally during summer and hunting season. Sometimes trappers use them during the season, but as far as I know there are no year-round dwellers on the river between here and Glenora, 140 miles up-river.

Besides the cabin on Sergief are the remains of a large barn, a milk house, and a machine shed. We had hoped, before actually moving here, to be able to restore these buildings. In our plans, Lee would occupy the milk house as a "bachelor pad" and the barn would be re-roofed and re-built to use as a community building and dormitory for visitors. The machine shed would be transformed into a temporary cabin for Neal, his wife, Deveril, and their baby, Jacob. We later determined that most of these buildings were too far gone, so, except for the machine shed, we have simply used what materials we can salvage from them.

Neal immediately started to work on his cabin. He raised the building to provide room for a floor well above ground level, put in windows, and built partitions. Lloyd and Lee quickly raised a storage building near our cabin, where we put most of the equipment and furnishings we'd brought with us. The better pieces of furniture we stored in the attic of the cabin. They are still there — waiting.

After getting most things under cover, Lloyd turned his attention to the cabin itself. Rotting floorboards were torn out, big recycled windows installed, walls sheathed with grooved plywood, cupboards built and a sink installed. The back porch was rebuilt and closed in, with the washing machine installed. The attic was floored sufficiently to enable us to use it as a bedroom.

This, however, wasn't all accomplished those first few months; it took place over the course of a year or more.

While all the first flurry of activity was going on we were also tilling ground and planting a garden, mostly with plants I'd started in Wrangell earlier in the spring. We were also trying to work around one another, sleeping and eating together in the main cabin. There were Lloyd, me, Lee, Jeff, Sethnie, Neal, Deveril and Jacob — not to mention two large dogs, Smeller and Sophie, and Taffy, a little red miniature dachshund.

When we finally got the new cookstove uncrated and set up, things got a little easier, but in July it started to rain — every day for forty days. The mosquitos were unremitting in their attack. The no-see-ums (small biting gnats) came out of the soil in clouds. We found that the only way we could tolerate turning the soil was with a smoky bonfire or smudge pot burning. Then there were the "big boys," huge flies that came by the hundreds to gorge on any unprotected flesh. A bite from one actually leaves you bloodied. Many a time one of us would rear up from a task, clutching the afflicted spot with a cry of mingled anguish and anger. Since we had no screening, we were usually forced to cook over the hot wood stove with no ventilation. We didn't dare open the door. Bug repellent and killer became big items on our shopping lists.

One hot day Jeff cut a heavily weed-covered area with a machete as he prepared it for tilling. Because of the heat he stripped down to his pants. That evening all his exposed skin started to itch; his eyes swelled and ran with tears. I applied calamine lotion, but by morning he had small water-blister-like lesions over a good share of his upper body. It seems he'd been sprayed by the juices of the Indian celery plant, to which some people are especially sensitive. Caladryl lotion gave him relief, but the scars stayed with him for several weeks. Whenever I suggest any weed cutting these days he's careful to cover up and use a kerchief over as much of his face as possible. I thought I was immune until a year or so later when I got my initiation after using the weed-cutter. Now I, too, am a buttoned-down, neckerchief-wearing worker.

Everything we did seemed to take more money, material and time than we'd anticipated. Everything was going out — nothing coming in. Conditions were trying; nerves got edgy. We discovered there's a lot more involved in a move such as ours than simply finding a place you love and moving in. It takes real organization to live on the bounty of the wilderness around you — especially if you feel you really should have more than an 8 by 10 cabin, oiled paper windows, and a sack of flour with a supply of jerky. It's easy to romanticize about the expectations of our early-day pioneers and mountain men. It's something else to try to approximate those experiences, even in a limited way.

Bathrooms, or their equivalent, can come up for lively discussion in a wilderness inhabitant's plans. Deveril decided that, for her, a bathroom was a must. My plans are definitely still in the future. The little old outhouse still sits out back. It's been moved a time or two, but nothing has replaced it. Often, at first, when we were still apprehensive about the possibility of attack by wild animals, there would be considerable hesitancy about making that last trip at night.

"Mom, will you go with me?" Sethnie would ask. So off we'd go, flashlight beams probing the bushes. While Deveril was still here, she and Sethnie usually went together.

Baths and showers are actually a more critical issue. The old tin tub leaves a lot to be desired. Difficult, you might say, to stretch out and relax in one of those gadgets, especially if you're worrying that someone will forget and come around your towel-draped chair in front of the tub. I rely mostly on sponge baths, which are efficient if not as esthetically pleasing as other ways of bathing. Outside bucket showers are easy enough to rig up, but it's not often that the weather is warm enough to make the thought enjoyable.

I still want a real bathroom — with lots of hot water — and one of these days it will probably be here. More house space is the first hurdle to overcome.

When we make that addition we plan for the toilet to be a composting type. We aren't sure how our present water system would support the repeated flushings of a regular toilet. Also, I like the idea of the wastes being used in an acceptable fashion, rather than sent off into the ground water or river.

For the present, I remind myself that most of the world still uses accommodations as, or more, primitive than mine. There are times, too, when I hear some fine vocalizations coming from the outhouse: voices that I never hear anywhere else. The comfrey plants around it grow lushly, too — speaking of silver linings.

Early on we made plans as to how the cabin would be enlarged — the excavations for the footings were even dug. I had visions of raising the roof to give headroom for two bedrooms in the attic, complete with dormers. But the excavation work is all that's been done; it simply hasn't worked out the way we planned.

Well — I have a different site picked out now and plans for a lodge-type building, its back to the huge stone wall nearby, its front providing a terrace with easy access to the boat tie-up.

Strange as it may seem in such a rainy, cloud-covered area, I'm convinced that passive solar heating could be of real value to us during the months when we need heat most. In the months of December through March we experience lots of clear sunny weather that could be used to our advantage. The tentative plans we've drawn up utilize the sun, earth berms in the rear, and fuel storage and furnace in a ground-level, daylight basement.

When you first move into remote country your concerns are shelter, water and heat. The shelter, after a fashion, was here; water was available; we were surrounded by forests for fuel. The trick was getting the water and wood to the house.

With the heavy rainfall in Southeast Alaska and the abundance of water usually on the ground, it would seem that providing a suitable water supply would never be a problem. Such is not the case. Even in the nearby small cities of Southeast a scarcity of water develops when they go without rain for thirty days or so. Admittedly, this doesn't happen very often, but it can be a cause of real concern. It can be a concern on Sergief, too.

Of the two sources of water on the island, one is a large spring quite a distance from the cabin. It had been encased and was evidently once used as a water supply for the barn and milk house. The water must come from deep in the ground, because often it will remain unfrozen or with only a thin crust of ice long after the ground is deeply frozen. Because of the distance we have never used it, but Neal once planned on getting his water from it.

The water supply closer to us is a small spring coming out of a ravine in back of the cabin. Its sweet, clear water always runs in even the coldest of weather.

When we arrived the water was filtering down the draw through a large pipe, to be deposited in a rotting wooden barrel. From there it was delivered into a plastic pipe via a hole in the barrel, to run to the cabin whenever the amount of water in the barrel was enough to insure sufficient pressure for it to reach its destination.

During the first spell of hot weather that first summer the trickle of water became alarmingly small. Much of it evaded the barrel and was wasted in runoff. We found ourselves, increasingly, having to take our pans and buckets to the draw to get our water at the source. It became difficult to keep clean; baths in the 34 °F water of the river took a hardy soul indeed. If our hair seemed a trifle gritty, it could be explained by the silt the river carries during that time of the year. Of course, our shortage of water was soon remedied by the following weeks of rain. And our trips to the spring weren't all that bad. It's a pleasant place: cool, overhung by willows, with the sound of running water soothing one's senses. It afforded a time to stop, wait for the bucket to fill, and look at the beauty.

Deveril and I learned to work together that summer, to love and respect one another in a way that has survived the five years since. When she and Neal decided, later in the summer, that for financial reasons it was imperative they go out to find work, with great sadness I saw them go. At that time they still intended to come back and eventually live here. And they did come back each fall for two years to work on their cabin, but eventually they became established in Wrangell, bought a house, and increased their family with a baby girl. I understand their reasons and reasoning, but it was the loss of one more plank of the platform on which my life was based in coming here, and I still wish I could see Jacob coming down the trail to catch frogs.

In mid-fall it became evident that it was necessary for Lloyd to return to Washington on business. Winter was coming and we still had wood to get. The repairing of the water system was postponed; we learned to live with the set-up. With the first freezes the plastic pipe froze and was just too much work to keep thawed; it was easier to go to the barrel. It wasn't too long before even that was frozen and we were reduced to taking our buckets and dishpans to the beach on each high tide, when the fresh water was pushed close by the tide over the ice.

I didn't hear any complaints from the kids. It gave Jeff and Sethnie a break from their studies and Lee and me a reason to get out of the house. We could always laugh as we made our relay to hand up the containers. We made sure we left full pans on the drainboard at night in case of fire. We were also careful to keep fire extinguishers handy.

The next year Lloyd and Lee built a large holding tank for the water and buried the pipe below frost line; that took care of our water problems. The second winter, however, when it was so cold we felt we should leave the water running to keep it from freezing, we got up one morning to a shock. The intake pipe hadn't frozen. No, it was still dripping away. But the drain had frozen, the sink had run over, and the kitchen was an indoor skating rink with ice an inch thick on the floor. Added insulation has saved us from having to leave water running anymore. Insulation under the floor and in the ceiling has made a lot of difference to the warmth of the cabin. We don't have to worry about the firewood freezing to the floor these days.

Wood, the first winter, was something of a problem. Lee and Neal had cut quite a bit during the weeks they were here alone, but a lot of it was green — willow and alder growing around the place — and some driftwood from the beach. There was a lot of driftwood then, nobody had used much for years, but most of it was cottonwood. If you've never used cottonwood, I don't recommend you try. Dry, it burns like paper; wet, it hardly burns at all. It's a spongy, porous wood I have to be desperate to use. The only thing I've found that I really like it for is smoking fish. About half dry and barked, it does a good job, producing clouds of aromatic smoke.

While there's some alder on the island, it's not abundant and it's mostly small. Spruce is the fuel of choice. The whole island, except for the marsh flats, is covered with it, and if we're lucky it comes floating down-river into the cove.

The first fall we knew we had to increase our supply before snow covered the land. Lee cut down two trees so they fell toward the cabin from higher up the bank behind us. He took over (and has kept) most of the responsibility for the wood supply. Since we had no mechanized equipment it was easier to bring the wood down the hill than try to wheelbarrow it up from the beach. Jeff worked on the wood too, splitting and stacking, and I had to laugh when I noticed him keeping an eye on how much I was burning in the cookstove. The wood had to be split fairly small and took a lot of work, so I really couldn't blame him. We learned that spruce limbs are especially hard, and are an excellent fuel to hold a long fire. During the coldest nights we stoked up the cookstove — as well as burned the heater — with the limbs; and in the morning the teakettle would be cheerfully humming away, the wood reduced to a thick bed of red coals almost like a coal fire.

In the intervening years we've learned to take our fuel almost exclusively from the bounty of the river. It's not unusual for one of us to run for the field glasses and holler out, "There's a good spruce coming down-river." Lee runs for the skiff, makes a dash for the log and pulls it in before it gets too far out on the flats. Sometimes a high tide will even deposit a fat spruce right in the cove. They're continually being dislodged by erosion from the banks of the river, so the supply is fairly constant, especially during those months of the year when melting snows raise the water level of the river. I sometimes entertain myself by imagining where a particular log might have come from: Andrew's Slough; Shake's Glacier; the Iskut River; or maybe way up around Telegraph Creek.

Usually sometime in summer, Lee, or Jeff if he's here, takes the boat and saw and goes up-river to where a few logs might be bunched on a sand bar, cuts off the root wad and limbs, and tows home a small raft of logs. It's part of the security of the wilderness to know that the heat of many a good fire is just waiting for you to go get it. Who could ask for more? Isn't that just as good as earning the money in some other way to purchase the same net product?

There is a program of free wood for Alaska residents, administered by the U.S. Forest Service. Other states with national forests also have free-use programs, but they are more restrictive. Here, each Alaska resident eighteen or older may take up to ten thousand board feet of timber out of the national forest each year — as long as they abide by the rules. This timber may be used for any purpose the taker chooses except financial gain. It may be used as logs, lumber or wood; and may be spruce, cedar or hemlock. Houses, additions, garages and sheds in Wrangell have been built with this timber.

We have had no reason, yet, to avail ourselves of this program, but since there's no cedar or logs of a suitable size for log buildings on Sergief Island, we may in the future. It would entail getting the logs to the water, making a raft of them, and pulling them across the flats on high tide. Not too insurmountable.

We also hope to set up a portable sawmill to make the lumber for most of our needs.

As I sit and look out my window on this winter day, my heart is filled with gratitude for the view of water, snow, and ice in front of me. The privilege of living and learning here these past five years has been a great one. Beauty and the power of nature is all around me.

I heard on the radio today that our present world population of 4.5 billion is expected to double by 2025. Well — I'll probably be gone by then, but my children won't, and I'd like them to be able to feel the exhilaration that comes from knowing that for miles around you there's wilderness, populated by animals in their wild state. Living here as we do I can still feel joy when I see a boat coming into the cove. I'm not surfeited with humanity like so much of mankind; I'm sincerely happy to see them coming. We need feel no apprehension when strangers come into the yard. They've all been invited in to sit, eat, or spend the night if need be. Some of them have stayed overnight, although our accommodations lack elegance.

Alaska isn't paradise. The rate of crimes of violence is high, most of them associated with alcohol or drugs. Long hours of darkness, boredom, and high unemployment can heighten nervous tension. However, it's one of the few places left on earth where people are scarce enough to still need and, usually, appreciate each other. Even the state offers help and encouragement to its residents that's found nowhere else that I know of. I appreciate Alaska and would like to think that during my sojourn here I'll be able to add something of value for those who will come after.

Jeff poses with his first bear.

III

GROWING, FINDING AND CATCHING DINNER

When a touch of warmth is felt in the air, when the ice has melted off the grounds around the cabin and run in rivulets to the beach, when the ravens are doing their mating ballets over the cabin accompanied by the beautiful cascading cry of the eagle — I know it's spring, and time to plan for the growth of all things lush and bountiful.

There's really little I'd rather do. The compost pile is uncovered, fluffed, sifted (rescuing as many of the angleworms as possible in the process) and mixed with soil and perlite for the seed flats that will go onto the wide board windowsill. Early cabbage, broccoli, cauliflower, all get their start. Soon some early corn gets a headstart along with cucumbers, squash and celery. Because I'm an optimist I start tomatoes, peppers and petunias, although I've never had great success with any of the three.

We came here with the hope and intention of learning to provide and produce as many of life's necessities as possible. That made one of the criteria for our parcel of land to be enough good garden soil to produce a year's supply of vegetables. Since Southeast Alaska is primarily a system of heavily wooded hills and mountains interspersed with fjords, flatter pieces of land are scarce and are often muskeg: bogs formed by decaying vegetation because of lack of drainage, often shallowly overlying rock. The heavy rains leach nutrients and carry off what topsoil there is.

There is much variance in the amount of rainfall received by the towns in the Panhandle, from around 160 inches at Ketchikan to a mere 40 inches at Skagway. We in the Wrangell area usually get in the neighborhood of 80 inches. That's a lot of rain, but coming, as we did, from a part of western Washington that gets 40 to 50 inches a year, it isn't as traumatic to us as it might be to lots of folks. For one thing, we don't get lots of gray, cloud-covered days here. It's either raining hard, getting in its quota, or the sun breaks through in a glorious brilliance that even the most jaded heart must rejoice in. The winters on the Stikine (with a few notable exceptions) are cold and clear, the sun shining off the ice in patterns of gold. When the cold winds and rains of late winter break the ice and send it crashing into the cove, even that is an adventure and lesson in the power of nature.

Sergief Island shares with Farm Island and some other spots on the Stikine River the enviable reputation of possessing some of the best growing land in the area. When I first dug my hands into its deep brown loaminess I was sure the reputation was deserved.

For years there had always been a garden on Sergief, put in and maintained on weekends, or other free time, by various Wrangell residents. A half-acre piece of land up by the old machine shed had always been used. The first year we used it too, and had a reasonably good garden, although moving here in June gave us a late start — even with seedlings.

Neal and Jeff tilled, cleared wild berry bushes, and put up supports, while Deveril, Sethnie and I planted seeds and plants and hauled water for the young plants from the second spring by the old barn.

That June was hotter and drier than any June since we've been here. I enjoyed it but so did the mosquitos; they came out in force. Jacob was one year old and a favorite target. His soft little arms and legs were a welter of bites, but even so, he enjoyed his time in the dirt of the garden. It was hard on his mama, however.

The next fall we cleared a plateau of nearly flat land closer to the cabin. It was covered, head high, with salmon and thimbleberry bushes that seemed a formidable prospect, but we cut and burned and proved the worth of our new Troy tiller by churning the bushes up, roots and all. Jeff manned the tiller, Sethnie and I picked up sticks and roots. When we finished the spot in time to plant a cover crop of winter rye, we were filled with pride and a real sense of accomplishment.

It's much handier for me to work there, going back and forth to the cabin. I'd often wondered, too, if a berry-eating bear might consider me an interloper as I followed the trail through the berry bushes to the upper garden.

I have to admit this isn't the best climate for gardening. Hot, sunny days are not to be taken for granted. When the seed catalogs give an estimated number of days to maturity, you can easily add half again as many. This is a cool, coastal climate with all its problems and limitations. I've learned to practice what I call "defensive gardening."

An early start, for many plants, is imperative, yet if you place seeds in cold, wet soil they may very well rot. If you wait too long your crops never mature. I've learned that a soil thermometer serves me well. Plants I've started indoors are kept until the weather stabilizes in late May. Waiting until the soil warms offers some protection, also, from the root maggots that are our only serious pest.

I practice basic organic gardening, but my dislike of pesticides fades when I go out to find my early broccoli, cauliflower and cabbage being systematically destroyed by nasty little beasties.

Last year I started an early seed-flat of these vegetables in the house. Later I started more in the cold frame by the porch. In May I set out a row of fine sturdy plants. They were thriving until I went up, one day, to find one wilted with a reddish hue. Pulling it up, I found its roots devoured by root maggots. I'd set these plants out with high hopes because they all had collars of sawdust to discourage flies from laying their maggot-producing eggs. The plants were also drenched by a solution of Bug-2:Seek, a product consisting of microscopic life forms called *Neopectana carpocapsae*, which attack and parasitize the soft-bodied maggots.

After about the third day, with my plants being knocked down like bowling pins, I panicked and hauled out the Diazinon. Even that didn't stop the attack, and I failed to save even one. We had no broccoli, cauliflower or cabbage from our garden last year until the late-planted ones matured — with no particular protection. Even these were not good heads. As they felt the shortening days they reacted accordingly, rushing into maturity before reaching a good size.

Last year we had an especially cold, rainy summer, which made life difficult for some of the plants, but we had beautiful peas, carrots and other root crops, and the best potato crop we've ever had.

Most vegetables are planted in raised beds — usually about three feet wide. This allows the soil to warm faster as well as shed water. After the beds are made, those that will be planted with heat-loving plants are covered with clear plastic. The clear plastic heats the soil faster than black, and, while it allows a few weeds, they're easily removed. Corn, squash, cucumber, beans and tomatoes are all planted in holes in the plastic. Cucumbers and tomatoes also have a plastic covering over their tops.

I've had good luck with cucumbers by covering them with a half-cover that catches the sun's rays and bounces them back onto the plants. 'Victory', a gynoecious (all female) variety, and 'Sweet Slice', a Japanese type, have given me good yields, lots for fresh use and even enough for pickles, though these aren't sold as pickling varieties.

The backbone of the garden in most of Alaska is the root crop — carrots, beets, parsnips, potatoes. On Sergief we rarely have a failure in these vegetables regardless of what the weather does. The deep, sandy loam is excellent for the long roots, and since they aren't demanding in their needs they're a pleasure to grow.

Beet greens are one of the first garden offerings to grace our table in spring. They've been preceded, of course, by the first tips of the wild stinging nettles that grow in large patches. When gathered (with gloves on my hands), washed and steamed quickly, nettles come to the table with an acceptance that had to be earned from some of the family. Nettles are rich in protein, fiber, vitamins and mineral. The growing tip is tender and flavorful well into summer.

Each year I've learned more about getting a quality crop of a good variety of vegetables, and I'm still learning. It's a fascinating project — to me at least — and a worthwhile one, too. Practically all the produce consumed in Southeast Alaska is shipped here by barge or ferry over thousands of miles from place of growth. I'd like to see the whole country, Alaska in particular, eating food produced close to the point of consumption. Think of the savings in money, energy and nutrients.

Since coming here we've planted raspberries, four varieties of strawberries, rhubarb and asparagus. We've also planted a young orchard, and last fall I harvested a few apples off the young 'Harolson' tree.

This isn't fruit tree country, so while all the trees are healthy and growing we have yet to see whether or not they'll ever give us a year's fruit supply. Last year most of them had lots of blossoms but pollination was a problem, so I may have to become a beekeeper. That might not be bad.

Everything we plant is the hardiest, earliest-maturing variety of that particular plant we can find: 'Earli-V' and 'Polar-V' corn, 'Salad Bowl' lettuce, 'Victory' cucumbers, 'Siberian' tomatoes, 'Lincoln' and 'Douglas' pear trees, and 'Northern Star' cherries are only a few examples. It's a challenge and it's fun.

Rodale Press, besides its many good publications, is also active in promoting "The Cornucopia Project." This project helps groups become active in setting up information centers and distribution of locally grown crops, in hopes that any who choose may become more self-sufficient. In a world of hunger and uncertain supplies of many things, self-sufficiency, especially the knowledge of how it can be attained, is a goal well worth working toward.

* * *

Southeast Alaska is probably one of the easier spots on earth in which to be self-sufficient. There are abundant berries, mushrooms, and seaweed; salmon, halibut and bottom fish, all for the taking once you've learned the skills involved; shellfish and crustaceans are readily available; moose and deer, while not exactly waiting for you, are there to be had.

Wild berries are plentiful. Up-river, great patches of highbush cranberries grow along the banks. One of our favorite fall excursions is to go into the wilderness to pick cranberries. They grow on bushes up to eight feet tall, the berries in clusters easy to strip. They are a tart-flavored red berry with one large flat seed. While best gathered around the time of the first frost, they aren't damaged easily by weather and often hang on the bush all winter. Often when we're out on our Christmas tree-cutting jaunt we'll refresh ourselves by sucking and chewing a cluster of frozen highbush cranberries. While not genuine cranberries they do have a similar flavor.

I use most of mine to make juice and jelly. They also make a ketchup that goes especially well with game. The juice, sweetened and diluted, is very good by itself, but is a special treat when mixed with ginger ale. It also makes an exceptional sherbet.

Since lowbush cranberries don't grow on Sergief Island I rarely pick them. They're plentiful on Wrangell Island, however, and are used in the same ways as the commercial cranberry.

Salmonberries seem to grow wherever nobody disturbs them. There are several big patches on Sergief and when the spring weather is good they outdo themselves in production. There are both red and the typical salmon-colored varieties. They're tender, tasty berries that make good jam and pie. If you like something special, carefully cook a whole-berry preserve.

Last year they were discovered by a great flock of robins that stayed until the last one was gone. I didn't like it much but I liked the bright-eyed raiders so I tolerated their big appetites. Once the salmonberries were gone the robins stayed around a day or two to hunt my unwary angleworms, then left without even saying thank-you. That was the first year they'd come in such numbers.

Blue huckleberries and blueberries (I have a hard time telling the difference) grow plentifully on Wrangell Island, often on logged-off areas. They're probably my favorite wild berries. Sethnie and I can pick five gallons or more in a day, enough to give us a year's supply of jam plus berries for pie and muffins. They make a delicious pie — worthy of long anticipation.

Thimbleberries, red, flat-cupped berries, grow here plentifully. They make good jams but aren't a favorite of mine. If the spring rains are heavy they are subject to a blight that makes them unpalatable.

Elderberries are plentiful, growing wild on nearly every bank around the cabin area. Elderberry is an attractive, pleasantly scented shrub when in bloom; as the fruit ripens it attracts birds in great numbers. Often, in summer, I can stand before the sink and be entertained by a flock of wild canaries eating their fill at the bush outside the window. That bush is never harvested; it's left for the birds. Different kinds of birds keep coming until the last berry is gone.

The berries I strip from the other bushes go into the juicer/steamer to make juice for drinks, jelly and syrup. I also make a jam and meat relish we enjoy.

The red variety that grows here is reportedly not tolerated by some people; it causes digestive upsets. We, however, have never suffered any ill effects from all we've used; any color growing nearby may be used.

There are some wild black currants, which I'm told are not common, on Sergief Island. They spread attractively over the rocks along the beach. An afternoon's picking gives an afternoon's diversion as well as the fruit — that is, if you're a berry picker at heart. I can pick away, the sun on my back, mind free for all the things that are fun to think about. A companion or two makes it all the better. The black currant makes a delicious conserve, left slightly thin, laced with walnuts. Try serving it over your sourdoughs with a dollop of sour cream!

* * *

Many wild mushrooms grow at various times of the year here. I recognize only a few of the choice ones, and am working on enlarging my selection. "Bear bread" is impossible to mistake: It grows in plentiful orangey ledges on trees and is tenderest early in the summer. Usually only the outer edge is used, as the thicker portion is tough and woody. All varieties of mushroom must be gathered while very young because they deteriorate rapidly and become infested with insects. Drying is probably the best way to preserve them for winter use.

* * *

Free gifts come from the sea in the form of seaweed. The long bulbous type of kelp called bull kelp, because of its resemblance to a bull whip, makes excellent pickles when picked early in the year while the crop is young. After soaking, the tender rings cut from the stipe, or long stem, can be made into sweet or dill pickles, full of minerals.

Other types of seaweed are good and have long been a staple of Native Americans. They are dried and added in winter to stews and soups. I haven't yet learned to utilize this resource fully, partly because I have to go away from Sergief Island to gather seaweed. The waters around the island, except at high tide, are fresh, thereby doing us out of seaweed, as well as clams, oysters and other seafood. But it's only a few miles to go.

Sometimes after a good southerly blow and a high tide the beach will be littered with seaweed torn loose by the sea and swept over to us. Then I descend to the beach with my plastic bags to gather mulch for the garden. It adds precious minerals as well as making a weed-free protection for plants.

You may already be using kelp in your diet in the form of algin added to ice cream, chocolate milk, puddings and other prepared foods. It makes a smoothing, thickening agent.

* * *

Sometime in late February or early March — about the time the ice usually breaks out of the river — the hooligan make their first run up the river. The Indian name is "oolichan," where the word hooligan comes from (it's often spelled eulachon). These small smeltlike fish, rich in oil, were prized by Native Americans. By the millions they make their way up the Stikine, attended by thousands of gulls, eagles and ravens, all come for the easy repast. People come out from town with large nets that they use to catch great supplies. It's not unusual for a boat to go home carrying two fifty-gallon drums full of the small silver fish. Sometimes, if the ice is late in breaking up, they go up the river undisturbed, under the ice. There is, however, nearly always another, later run.

They're good, and if cooked so that oils can drain, will be crisp and brown. They're also good when smoked, and if you want to retain all the nutrients don't even bother to clean them. Simply wash and place on the racks for a few hours to produce a tasty lunch or snack.

Soon after the hooligan, a series of runs of various kinds of salmon take place. First appears the mighty king salmon, favorite of most people here. The kings are followed throughout the summer by runs of pinks, coho and sockeye. These fish don't feed as they go up the river to spawn, but Alaska permits netting under the subsistence laws in designated spots. It's easy enough to obtain a year's supply of fish in a few hours' time — fish to freeze, can and smoke.

Behind many houses in Wrangell you can see a small house. When you see smoke spiraling out of its vents you know it's not an outhouse. There are many methods of smoking fish, many preferences for differing recipes, which, though varying only slightly, produce real differences in the final product. I'm still learning.

Before coming here the closest I'd ever come to smoking fish was when I helped my dad gather wood for his little smokehouse. It isn't hard but there are lots of variables, such as how long you leave the fish in how strong a brine; how much smoke you give it from how hot a fire; how many hours over the smoke; and what variety of salmon. It all makes a difference. Last year I was well satisfied with my smoked salmon, even though I don't suppose it would stack up against some of our champion fish smokers in Southeast Alaska.

* * *

All this effort to produce and gather food would be wasted if the food were not properly taken care of: gathered quickly, processed with care, cooked with imagination.

We can, dry and freeze (when we're able), eating fresh for as long as possible. I've also taken a new look at raw foods, and include as many as possible in our diet. This becomes more difficult after we've been frozen onto the island for several months, but there are always sprouts to fall back on: alfalfa, mung, wheat and radish are only a few of what can be used.

It's important in a situation such as ours to keep meals varied and interesting as well as nutritious. To make that easier and quicker, I make many of my own home mixes: pancake, biscuit, cake and others. We always have our own homemade yogurt; the sourdough pot is bubbling away, and is used more for pancakes and cakes (it makes a marvelous chocolate cake) than it is for bread; and the root cellar, come fall, holds a year's supply of potatoes, carrots, turnips, cabbage and parsnips, along with the winter's supply of staples from town. We have made every effort, these last few years, to have all this in by the end of October. You may have plenty of time after that — then again, you might not.

* * *

When I lived in Washington state I made bread only occasionally. It seemed like a drawn-out process when I had other things I would rather do. So, though I've always enjoyed cooking, bread was never on my list of specialties — not that I didn't appreciate a good homemade loaf of bread.

When we moved to Sergief Island, bread became my sole responsiblity. Between being none too familiar with bread-making and being totally unfamiliar with the wood range, I had some interesting experiences.

One day during our first summer I had a batch of bread ready for the oven: whole wheat laced with wheat germ, soy flour, molasses and other good things, even a sprinkling of bone meal; the loaves were nicely rounded in the pans. The stove and the day were warm enough to make me anxious to get out of the kitchen. I placed the three loaves in the oven, shut the stove dampers and made for the door. About thirty minutes later, Sethnie came running, "Mom, something's coming out of the oven." As I pulled, the oven door opened with difficulty. The dough had overflowed its pans, partially sealing the door. The dough remaining in the pans was pale and sagging in the middle. I fixed the fire, finished baking the bread and had to set the pitiful mess on the table that night. There was no running to the store for a quick replacement to save my wounded pride.

Through trial and error I've learned a bit about baking bread. Almost any recipe will do; it's what you do with the recipe that counts. When the book says to knead for 8 to 10 minutes, it means it. No short cuts. Longer can never hurt, and if you spend that time figuring out some particular problem or coordinating each punch on the dough with pulling in the muscles of your abdomen, it isn't lost time. More kneading after the first rising makes for a lighter, finer-grained loaf, too. Do not allow the loaves to over-rise in the pans.

Oven temperature is extremely important. When first placing the loaves in the oven the temperature must be hot enough (around 400°F) to pull the loaves to their maximum size and hold them while a crust is formed with enough strength to give the loaf stability. Once this point is reached, oven temperature may be reduced to around 300°F to complete baking. If the loaves sound hollow when tapped, they're done.

If either of these points is neglected (lengthy kneading or too-low temperature at first) the result will be crumbly, full of holes, or flat.

I don't usually use a recipe anymore, except for a specialty bread. I start by measuring my hot water into the bowl and go from there. Each cup of water, 1 teaspoon salt, 1 tablespoon sugar or other sweetener, 1 tablespoon shortening will give you about one loaf of bread (depending on the size of the pans) when mixed with sufficient flour to make an easily handled dough. Other ingredients are added depending on my fancy. Sometimes all whole-wheat flour, sometimes white, but most often a blend of several different flours and grains, even the leftover oatmeal or other cereal from breakfast, is added along with anything else, like brewer's yeast and powdered milk, that I feel can be slipped in unobtrusively. The only caution is not to have too high a percentage of non-wheat grains, or the gluten will not be developed, giving, again, a crumbly loaf. Oh yes, I've gotten so I can open that oven door with a reasonable degree of confidence.

* * *

Another small thing I've found especially useful is a method of canning zucchini and a few other vegetables. The idea came from a letter written to *Family Circle* magazine a few years ago. I've used it ever since with success and pleasure.

Slice enough zucchini to fill a gallon container, cover the vegetables with water and add 6 tablespoons good cider vinegar and 2½ tablespoons salt. Bring to a boil until the vegetables change color, pack into hot, sterile jars, seal with sterile lids, and that's it! I've used it on all types of summer squash and other vegetables I intend to fry later or use in a casserole requiring further cooking. It is not meant to be used when the vegetable will be simply heated and served.

* * *

On the northeast end of the island lies a meadow once homesteaded and farmed by a lone man who, I am told, lost his life there one cold winter after his cabin burned down. Only an old hay rake left in the meadow memorializes his years there.

Around the rake grows an abundant crop of mint that I enjoy harvesting in the summer months. I walk among the grasses, rich with the purple blossom of the mint and other blooms, and dream my thoughts: memories, I sense, that were never really mine, but inherited by me from peoples and cultures here long before my short day.

The mint is brought home, slowly dried on a rack over the wood stove, mixed with comfrey, chamomile, raspberry and strawberry leaves, red and white clover blossoms, or any number of other herbs. I have a mixture designed for a morning wake-up cup; one for a relaxing bedtime cup.

Putting the blends together is a pleasant, fragrant job. Sethnie and I spread the dried materials on the big old table and work companionably together.

I estimate that for about $40 I could buy enough tea of all kinds and flavors to supply our family for a year. The varieties these days are many and enticing. Surely my hourly wage in tea preparation and many of the other food-producing activities is reduced to pennies. Most North Americans have been conditioned to the idea that "time is money," and feel slightly embarrassed, as if we're of little worth, if much of our time is spent in activities giving us little monetary gain. Someone has said that "Time is a gift." I agree. If my time here can be used to plant, grow or produce something where once there was nothing, I'm content.

On a rather brisk day, Joy gets out the wash.

IV

CLOTHES AND HOUSEHOLD EQUIPMENT

The years here have taught us that many of the things we used to think necessary are not, and vice-versa. Because we were moving to ALASKA we associated it in our minds with COLD. (Much of it is — places in interior Alaska, such as Fairbanks, and even parts of western Alaska, like the Kodiak chain.) Southeast Alaska, however, is relatively mild, rarely getting as cold as Chicago or many other places in the Lower 48. We don't get more rain, either, than a lot of places along the southern coasts. It just seems that way. The combination of northern latitudes and heavy precipitation gives a climate that, while mild, is sometimes trying.

I have no real quarrel with the climate except when I'm lonesome for some hot summer sun, or the rain rots my strawberries on the vine.

Anyway, when we were shopping for clothes to bring with us we went a little heavy on mukluks (heavy, felt-lined, rubber and leather boots) and black wool underwear. Both of these items can be useful at times, but they're usually not essential. Layering porous, lightweight wool socks and underwear is usually better than one heavy item.

Shopping for items in preparation for a whole new way of life can be fun, and most of us found it so. We skittered around, trying to keep in mind everything we'd learned from our wilderness survival books and magazines. While we got rid of things we felt unnecessary, we accumulated mountains of other things to bring with us.

Jeff studied his books and picked out his traps, snares and bottles of musky-smelling lures. Rain gear, heavy boots and underwear completed his preparations along with a couple of good knives (Buck and Gerber), and a sharpener and stone. Jeff and Lee both have found plastic-lined Army surplus wool pants to be warm, dry and serviceable. The surplus store is a good place to look first for your needs. If it's not there it's easy enough to look elsewhere.

Lloyd invested much of his shopping energy in buying powder, slugs, and other supplies for his re-loading equipment. Being already fairly well endowed with boots and underwear, he lay in a supply of heavy shirts and let it go at that. We've since found that, as work shirts, foam-lined flannel gives exceptionally good wear. I don't see them in the outdoor catalogs so maybe they're not macho, but they're light, warm, quick-drying and durable.

Sethnie and I both found we needed warmer coats as we drove through the bitter cold of a December in British Columbia, so in Prince Rupert we bought coats. For Sethnie we purchased a mid-thigh length down-filled coat with heavy twill shell. It was a good, durable investment that lasted until she outgrew it. I washed it carefully even though the tag said to dry clean. Since there are no dry cleaners in Wrangell we sometimes resort to desperate measures.

For myself, I bought a mid-weight polyesterfill nylon coat of over-the-hip length. It was serviceable and kept me warm enough, although I still intend to buy a really good coat — one of these days. When you consider that a top-quality coat costs in the neighborhood of $200, it bears thinking about.

Before moving, I bought at half-price a pair of insulated work boots that I've worn regularly over the five years we've been here, and they're still in good shape. The instructions that came with them said to never apply oils or other dressings, and I haven't. Even though I've sloshed for hours through the waters on the marsh flats they've never leaked — yet. They're an American-made product — we're still manufacturing some good things.

We tried to include in our provisioning some recreational equipment: water and oil paints, carving tools, embroidery kits, plenty of books and music. Some proved invaluable; others have yet to be used.

One piece of advice I'd offer to anyone contemplating a drastic change of life style would be to under-buy, rather than overdo it. Often your ideas of what you need or want will be very different after you've been in the new area awhile. You can learn a lot by observing how the locals get by.

Also, I find great pleasure in browsing through the wealth of catalogs that come through the mail. If you've already spent your allowance it's not much fun. Catalogs take the place, for me, of the large shopping malls that pleasured many a day.

You have to plan how to keep warm and dry. Anything that will do that for you is fine, whether it's from the finest outdoor shop or catalog or put together from items picked up at the Salvation Army. I've learned that the more things I can be thrifty about, the more room I have to splurge on something I really want.

Out here on Sergief Island we can go for weeks without seeing anyone outside of the family, so if we have patches on our Sears jeans it doesn't matter. Of course, Sethnie and Jeff have to have name-brand "in" jeans to wear to Wrangell.

* * *

An insulated, floatation-type work suit is one thing everyone who spends much time on northern waters should have. These suits are rainproof, wind-breaking, and will keep you afloat in cold waters for a few hours, if need be. Survival suits are good, too, but their use is limited. Since you can't work in them (they have hands, feet and hoods, all leak-proof), you must have sufficient notice of emergency to get into them. For our particular situation, a floating work suit offers adequate protection. Usually.

On the ninth of January, 1983, Sethnie and Lee took the small aluminum skiff and went to Wrangell. The ice was out of the river (it had been a winter of intermittent freezing and breakups); both Sethnie and Lee were anxious to get off the island for a while.

The outgoing trip was uneventful. They spent the day in town and stayed that night at Neal and Deveril's. Their intention of coming home the following day was thwarted by cold, windy weather with gusts of 45 miles per hour. Nobody should be on the Stikine River flats in that kind of weather; in a small skiff it's impossible. On the tenth we had a foot of new snow. By the eleventh the kids began to get over-anxious to get home. On January twelfth the tide occurred around noon. Since the water is smoother before full tide, and it's safer to be on the flats on a rising tide, they planned to leave Wrangell about 10 A.M., weather permitting.

Lloyd and I watched the weather that morning, and when we saw snow flurries building up we assumed they'd wait another day. They carried a CB radio on the boat, but we heard nothing from them or the folks in Wrangell. Visibility was poor so we could barely see Wrangell Island, let alone a small boat several miles out.

That evening, about 8 P.M., we called into Wrangell for Blue Belly (Lee), or Wildflower (Sethnie). Deveril came on the air. With tremulous voice she told us Lee and Sethnie had left Wrangell that morning. She had assumed they were home.

No words can convey my emotions at that moment. Sethnie and Lee . . . missing. Lost to the icy waters that have claimed so many lives?

It was dark; no one could mount a search until morning. We made periodic calls to them over the CB, hoping to make contact. Finally, about 11 P.M., a weak voice came over the air. It was Lee. Praise God they were both alive and safe, for the time being. They'd become disoriented in the snow, gotten into an ice pack, and had only just managed to fight their way onto the mainland. Wet and cold, they were only a few miles from home but very far in accessibility. The temperature was in the twenties (F). They were still in considerable physical danger. Lee had managed to start a small fire with the soggy fuel around him. He got Sethnie into the survival suit he carried on the boat, so, though wet, she finally managed to stop shivering. Lee had a work suit on, wet, but he assured us he was all right. It was a long night. We kept in regular touch and in the morning John Ellis, who has a large, tough aluminum boat, was able to push through the ice to get them and tow our boat to Wrangell. They stayed there a few more days until the weather moderated enough to permit safe passage.

That experience impressed me once more with the preciousness of the people around us. That survival suit may have saved Sethnie's life. At any rate, I give it credit. Each life is incredibly valuable.

* * *

Among our more important decisions when buying things preparatory to moving here was our selection of stoves. We looked, read, and did the best we knew, but it wasn't really enough.

1979 was still the era of the wood-stove boom. I think wood-stove popularity has cooled a bit since then, for several reasons. One is that getting your own wood can be quite a chore — a chore that's often next to impossible if you don't own your own wood lot. If you have to buy wood at current prices the savings are often negligible. Another reason for cooling enthusiasm, I believe, is the glowing "facts" given in the brochures of wood-stove manufacturers. When they give the hours the stove can be expected to hold on a filling of wood, or the number of B.T.U.s you can expect to enjoy, they're talking, I'm convinced, about perfectly seasoned hardwoods of the finest sort.

So if you, like me, don't live in the middle of a hardwood forest, or find yourself sometimes reduced to burning wood that is, admittedly, less than dry, you might feel your stove is not delivering exactly what you expected. You may even ask yourself if you've put all that money into a piece of junk, when the grates and liners burn out of your cookstove less than two years after you so proudly installed it in your kitchen, or when your beautiful new heater has a baffle as wavy as a five-foot sea, a split in its outer shell, and multiple cracks in its firebrick after the first hard winter.

All of this happened to us, and more, and though the stoves are still in use, if I ever get a chance to obtain new ones, I'll do it differently.

Regarding cast iron: I would urge future buyers to use any information available to them to check the quality of the cast iron in the stove they're considering. All cast iron is not created equal! In our family room in Washington state we had a hundred-year-old potbelly heater — no cracks in it — its grates still intact. I question whether many of the stoves manufactured today could last so long.

We wanted, mostly because of all the publicity touting the "new" age in wood stoves, to buy only air-tight stoves. To be able to slow combustion and hold fire is a distinct advantage, but I've found that the only time it can do us much good is when the weather is mild enough to require only a small amount of heat, or when, with the cookstove, I need only enough heat to keep a pot simmering. When the temperature drops down to the 20°(F) range, or less, we find the stoves aren't dampered down all that much. If you need a lot of heat you need a lot of oxygen. If the drafts are open the wood burns swiftly, so we use more wood than "efficient" woodburners are supposed to use.

When we shopped we looked at many brands and styles available in our area. We needed to take immediate delivery so couldn't wait for orders that seemed — at that time — to have a backlog of several months. Some of the more popular imports, like Jøtal, looked promising, but none of the companies' larger models were immediately available. For a heater, we finally settled for a Garrison, American-made rolled steel with double front-loading doors and firebrick lining. It's an attractive stove. The front doors allow it to be opened and used as a screened fireplace when desired (although it usually smokes). I don't want to be too hard on it. After all, we are still using it and it's five years old. But it doesn't perform as we were led to believe it would, and when we tried to exercise our rights connected with the twenty-year guarantee we found it singularly difficult. We were told we would have to have an estimate made by some qualified stove repairmen and submitted to the company for their consideration. If you can imagine what it's like to manhandle a heavy stove into and out of a boat you'll realize it could cause one to have second thoughts. I don't even know if there are any "qualified" stove repairmen in Wrangell, so the guarantees to people in remote spots can't necessarily mean all that they should.

Wood or coal-burning cookstoves hold an aura of nostalgia for most of us. They evoke mind pictures of cozy kitchens, the teakettle singing on the back of the range, a rag rug on the floor and a cat asleep under the stove. It's true, and I'm happy to have a wood cooking range — NOW. I didn't always feel so contented. They require some adjustments of the cook's mind.

After being used to continuous heat turned up or down by a dial, it takes a while to learn to remember to check the wood supply in the firebox regularly enough to avoid finding your fire out five minutes after you put the steak in the pan or the cake in the oven. You also must learn the best spot on the range for a particular pan.

My early childhood was spent in the company of wood ranges. I remember getting dressed in front of the open oven door, and my mother, brother, and I sitting with all our feet propped on that door one Christmas Eve as we tried to keep warm and my mother played hymns on her mandolin. At that rate I should have been prepared for wood range idiosyncrasies, but it had been a long time — and I wasn't.

When we shopped for a range we'd happened onto a business on the Olympic Peninsula, where they rebuilt and refurbished old stoves gathered from all over the country. Some of the stoves were gorgeous. The ornate old decorative pieces had been re-nickled; everything looked like new, except the design. "They don't make 'em like that anymore."

Emotionally I was sold on the spot, but my better judgment (and my husband) prevailed, so I regretfully turned away to look elsewhere.

There are attractive, well-built cast-iron stoves manufactured by Washington Stove Works, Portland Stove Foundry, Elmira Stove Works of Canada, and many others. We were able to look at many of them and finally settled for the Stanley, manufactured by the Waterford Company of Ireland. It appeared to be sturdy, of adequate dimensions — and it was airtight.

It wasn't my first choice. I'd have liked to buy the Finley Oval. It had a porcelain exterior, lots of nickel trim. It was beautiful . . . but it was also nearly $1000 more than the Stanley. So we bought the Stanley at a cost of $900 (I've since seen it advertised at close to $2000) and hauled it tenderly over the icy winter roads of British Columbia, barged it over troubled waters to Sergief Island, grunted it off the barge, up the bank, and into the cabin. It will undoubtedly be here forever.

Over the years I've learned to fry the potatoes without burning them, to shift the loaves of bread in the oven at the right time to keep from burning one side, to switch the layers of a cake from one rack to the other so they'll achieve their highest potential, to put more wood in the firebox before the fire goes out.

Levity aside, I'd like to take a crack at designing a cookstove. The oven would be *bigger* — they all seem to be about 20 by 20 inches — and the heat would be much more evenly distributed. I assume some stoves may be much better than others in the distribution of heat, but I'm afraid I may never have a chance to find out.

This past year we cast, of cement and fireclay, some panels to replace the burned-out ones in the firebox. The grates, too, are burned out and broken in places, but we haven't yet figured out what to do about them. So far, they're still holding the wood where it belongs.

So here I sit, sounding like an awful scold, while my poor little cookstove is warming the kitchen, doing all the good things a cookstove is supposed to do. After all, I'm not all that efficient either.

* * *

I like cooking gadgets, and some of my happiest hours have been spent perusing the Williams-Sonoma catalog and others of that breed. Oh, the positive flutter of heart that can accompany the sighting of a three-piece wok set, stainless steel fish poacher, or hammered copper Portuguese *cataplana* (used for cooking clam, fish, meat and vegetable dishes, so the ad says).

This does not even begin to describe the joy of dreaming of the possible purchase of sundae goblets (though we seldom have ice cream), melon bowls cunningly devised to look like cantaloupe shells, Chinese chicken pots, or heavy copper stock pots at $236 — on sale.

If I didn't suffer from a regrettable paucity of purse I'd probably buy much, but when we were getting ready to move here I often heard, "What do you need that for?" or "We don't have room for all that stuff." I can see now that we transported many things that would have better been sold at a garage sale. Then again, the fact that my best dishes, after five years, are still in their boxes in the storage shed doesn't make me wish I hadn't brought them — it just firms my resolve that one of these days I'll have a place to use and display them again. "All is vanity." Well?

I did dispense with some items I wished I'd kept. Among them is a vacuum cleaner. It may seem that a vacuum shouldn't be essential in a cabin of this size, and as I don't have one it would seem that it isn't. Nevertheless, the smoky dust can get heavy, and such places as under the heater are hard to reach with a broom. Sand from the beach would be much more easily cleaned up by a vacuum — even if I had to string the extension cord from the shed and start the generator.

A useful vacuum substitute that I brought with me is a carpet sweeper. It's well-made, does a good job, and its brushes are still good after years of use.

I kept my sewing machine and am glad. It's sometimes trying to time my sewing to coincide with other uses of the generator; that was another thing I had to get used to. Diesel fuel is expensive and difficult to haul up the beach, so we try to use it conservatively. Anyway, my sewing machine patches jeans, makes clothes for Sethnie and me, and helps with the making of Christmas gifts.

A lot of my electric appliances sit, unused, in the shed. I may as well have sold them, but I anticipated a different electrical system. A small hand mixer, other than the sewing machine, is the only appliance I use. An electric iron draws too much power. I have a gas iron that I don't like, so I iron little, and when I sew I do the necessary pressing with a heavy little old-style electric iron I keep hot on the cook stove.

If I had a "wish list" I suppose a refrigerator would top it, closely followed by a clothes dryer. We brought a refrigerator up here, but sold it in Wrangell when we saw how difficult it was going to be to provide a constant source of power for it. We plan — one day — to buy a propane-powered unit. They're available, but are relatively expensive. I've never seen a used one advertised. I remember the old Servel gas refrigerator in the first apartment Lloyd and I had after our marriage. If you turned the gas up a tad too high you froze everything in the box. Those old refrigerators seemed to last a lifetime, though. Oh, for one on Sergief Island!

For the time being I use, in cool weather, some shelves on the back porch as a cooler. This serves reasonably well since that room is kept just above freezing during all the winter months. Judicious opening of the door between kitchen and porch permits just the right amount of heat to escape to keep the food on the porch from freezing while not making a chill room of the kitchen, too. Sethnie, whose bed is on the north wall of the kitchen, complains that she sleeps in an icehouse. Once the weather moderates the door can be kept closed. That's the easy time. On hot days (there aren't too many of those) I find myself making repeated trips to the ditch that carries the runoff water from the spring, where a covered five-gallon bucket immersed in the icy flow keeps my bacon from getting moldy.

We do have a freezer. It runs on a "sometimes" basis. Even when it's in use, its position in a lean-to behind the storage shed doesn't exactly make it a convenience appliance. When we have a large supply of meat, in fall and winter, the freezer runs of necessity. The outside temperature, however, is low enough that the hours of operation are few. As the weather warms, requiring the generator to run more hours to keep the box at the proper temperature, we reach a point of diminishing returns. Then I use up or can all that remains in the freezer and it sits empty again until fall. This usually happens about the time the asparagus and strawberries ripen — causing me to complain bitterly.

One other reason for shutting it off is that we sometimes like to leave the island for two or three days during the warmer months. This would be impossible if there were food in the freezer.

For some generators you can buy an automatic-start device, so the generator will start on the demand of an appliance. Ours is not one of them. It should be easy to see that we need one . . . or other families on the island to share these tiresome little responsibilities. We probably wouldn't all want to take off at the same time — except on the Fourth of July!

On the subject of getting out the wash (and getting it back in the drawer), I'm the repository of much sage wisdom. First, when you move to the bush you don't need to get rid of your automatic washing machine, unless your water supply is severely restricted or you don't have running water at all.

I thought I had to have a gasoline-powered wringer washer so we bought a Maytag. I have no complaints about that machine. It does exactly what it's supposed to do and it's never needed any kind of repair except a couple of spark plugs. The thing is, I'm spoiled; I like an automatic washer and I don't like to hear the gasoline engine chugging away. I could as easily have plugged a washer into the generator power as anything else. It would have used more water but that ordinarily wouldn't make any difference.

I've found I can wash three or four loads of clothes in the same water and they're apparently as clean as with any other washing method. I also never heat water. The popular cold-water detergents really do get clothes clean in cold water. If you had a small baby you'd probably want to wash the diapers in hot water, but for us the cold works fine.

We get about eighty inches of rain, much of it in the warmer months of the year, so drying clothes does sometimes pose a problem — outside, that is. It's great when I can hang the clothes on the line, using the pulley to send them high in the air. Wind from the river catches them, imbuing them with whispers of fragrance from far-away places. Times when the rain comes steadily for days at a time cause me to stretch out the racks in the house — taking up a lot of the usable floor space. At those times I most wish for the whirling drum of the automatic clothes dryer, with the clothes tumbling out in fluffy perfection, ready to put on.

Well, I don't have a dryer, but I will one day — when we build a place to put it. It will be a gas model that requires electricity only to turn the drum. (Save the generator, you know.) And when the snow is four feet deep, or it's been raining for three weeks, I'll have my clothes-drying problems solved.

The first years we were here, when the family was still unscattered, I sometimes barely got one wash dried before I had to wash again. Damp jeans and underwear hanging from every available spot seemed permanent fixtures. With only Lloyd, Lee and me here it isn't such a problem . . . but I'd rather have the problem back.

Before closing this section I must tell you one of my favorite acquisitions since coming here. It's a Belgian waffler with deep holes to capture every bit of melted butter or sour cream. It bakes the waffles on top of the stove; temperature gauges on each side cooking them speedily to perfection. I like this gadget very much.

Oh, yes, a good word for tempered glass cookware. Although I've never seen it specially advertised for wood stoves, it should be. I was never particularly enamored of it on a gas or electric range, but I like it much better on the wood stove. It can be moved around on the top of the stove, it does a good job of evenly cooking the food, and it can come to the table with style.

After considerable deliberation I've decided my next household purchase will be a beautiful soup tureen. Think how impressive it will be to lift the lid on a fragrant tureen full of minestrone or chowder. I may even convert Lloyd to liking soup.

The tiller makes fast work of preparing the lower garden for planting.

V

POWER AND TOOLS

When you move to a remote and presumably simpler style of living you might feel that your power needs will be small enough not to require much consideration. Or you might, like me, study many books on alternative energy systems, assuming that you would have some such system in operation in short order. I would suggest that in the meantime, before making your move, you take a course in small engine repair. You just might need it.

There is something to be said for plugging into a community power source. When that's no longer available you find yourself faced with keeping a multitude of small engines in running order — unless you're determined to go entirely back to muscle power. It could be done, and in some ways would be simpler, but we live in a different age. We hear a different drummer. It's no simple matter to adjust our thinking away from the idea that we must have a power tool for all or most of our chores, or to accept the idea that it's okay to take a day to accomplish a job we're used to doing — with power — in an hour or two. Then there's the matter of whether you want to or not. Just how many of the hours of your life do you want to give to the goal of attaining that simpler life style? Or do you believe there's a reason, for yourself and others, to do just that; that perhaps the feeding and sustenance of the world depends on each human learning the best, least earth-destroying and depleting way of living in his little spot on the globe? Big, bigger, biggest, or fast, faster, fastest, doesn't necessarily equate with good, better, best; but where the line is crossed is something each person must determine for himself depending on his particular needs and personality.

Anyway, we haven't solved our energy needs on Sergief Island, and unless some new blood is infused into the lifeline around here it looks like things will stay that way.

Lloyd spent much of his life engaged in logging and the operation of heavy equipment, so his experience in motor repair stands us in good stead. Lee has welding experience that is invaluable in our situation. If we had to haul the power saw or generator into town for repair each time one of them had a problem we'd have a lot of downtime. Not that we have an inordinate number of breakdowns (some of our small motors have proven themselves remarkably trouble free), but each one requires its allotment of care and maintenance.

When we moved here we had tentatively decided to install — as we were able — a wind system capable of supplying power for our family. There's enough wind coming down out of the Stikine River basin to keep a propeller turning at a good clip most of the time. I'd still like to see a propeller turning out on the point. We've temporarily shelved the project because other needs seemed more urgent, and the cost isn't small. To buy and install a system that would handle our electricity needs would cost us a minimum of $12,000. Perhaps someone who was interested in scrounging and building many of the components could do it for a lot less.

There are many ways to produce power and I'm not an expert on any of them, but I'd like to be part of a team putting together a really efficient system for this particular place. Wind power seems like a good choice for electricity; water power offers possibilities; solar power is limited, with our many cloud-covered days; methane digesters sound interesting; and we're already utilizing wood power.

It seems to me that methane gas would be great as a source of power for lights, cooking, and running that clothes dryer I covet. I understand, too, that most diesel motors will accept a mixture of diesel and methane. Many small digesters are being used in India and China to give fuel for lights and cooking, besides adding great value as the slurry or sludge is returned to the soil to greatly enrich it. All we need now is the tank and paraphernalia and a few good cows to provide the manure. According to what I read it isn't really all that hard to set up.

The idea of producing our own alcohol for fuel purposes has crossed my mind, too. I have a patch of Jerusalem artichokes started that just might do as well as corn in the manufacture of alcohol for fuel.

All this doesn't give you much information except to let you know we haven't done a lot along the lines of alternative energy production. I wish it were different. Maybe someday we'll have a "Hasa" type building, sand-banked, fired by any kind of wood and rubbish, hot water coils in place, supplying heat and hot water to one or more homes. It sounds like a great idea to me.

There are many books on producing heat and power, written by experts in the field — people who have put many of these ideas into practice. There's even a company that sells kits to make various-size steam generators for power production of every sort. There's really no shortage of ideas and ways, but they do require a dedicated commitment to seeing them work.

In the meantime I'm stuck with my propane light in the ceiling and all of our small engines (I'm very glad to have them, too).

At present we have two generators: One is a Honda 400W portable; the other is a China Diesel Import, 3000W. They're both good items I don't hesitate to recommend. The Honda is small enough to carry down to the boat if a source of power is needed to recharge a battery. In the five years we've had it Lee has put new rings in it twice. I sometimes carry it down to the porch to power my sewing machine; it's good to have a backup source of power.

The China Diesel we've had about three years. It keeps our bank of batteries charged and gives enough voltage to turn a Skilsaw or other power tool. We run a twelve-volt television off it as well as a CB and radio. It could be utilized more than it is to supply twelve-volt lights, but we prefer to limit its use, to conserve diesel fuel and lessen wear on the machine. It's given us good use and has been virtually trouble-free except for vibrating its nuts and bolts loose. It needs to sit on a concrete slab.

The diesel engine came with a set of metric tools and enough parts to rebuild the engine once — at a price about one-half of its American-made counterpart. I don't like that fact, and I don't like not buying American, but there are forces at work much bigger than you or me — not including the wages paid to the American laborer.

Other tools that have given us good service are a Miller welder, a Troy seven horsepower tiller, and a Kioritz brush cutter. The welder was left over from Lloyd's heavy equipment days and has been in use many times since.

The tiller is good, heavy-duty, and starts easily. Last year it started on the first pull of the starter rope, after sitting all winter. We've had to do some repair work on it but most of those problems were brought about by our own mistakes.

It doesn't handle with quite the one-handed ease that's advertised. I'd like to see the little old lady in some of the ads manhandle one around a corner. This tool is not, in my opinion, easy to handle, so I avoid it whenever possible. Perhaps on perfectly level land maneuvering it would be easier, but I'd still have doubts about those corners.

The first year we got the machine it nearly paid for itself by preparing a 100 by 500-foot piece of new ground for planting the next year. It wasn't a piece of meadowland, but rather had salmonberry and thimbleberry cover of six feet or more, to say nothing of bracken fern and Indian celery with thick, deep roots. The Troy took it all in stride, although we went through and cut the tall brush, burning it as we went. I don't remember how many times Jeff went over the ground (Jeff probably remembers exactly), but all those roots didn't come up the first time over. With Jeff manning the tiller, Sethnie and I followed, gathering the roots he turned up and piling them to burn. It took us several days but the results were heart-warming. We stood and admired the deep brown soil and gave thanks for that pretty red Troy — even if it did take a strong arm to keep it in line.

The brush cutter has also done its duty with faithfulness, going before the tiller when necessary, preparing the area where the young orchard is planted, even doing double duty cutting grass when the lawn mower has been out of kilter. (We haven't had great luck with lawn mowers.)

When we first moved here Jeff seemed certain his lawn mowing responsibilities were over, once and for all. Lloyd and I looked around, however, and decided the looks and usability of the yard area would be improved by cutting the grass. Jeff grumbled that people living in the wilderness didn't need lawns. I had to concede his point, but we had to have a yard.

In some settings just a woodland garden of native plants would have suited me fine, but hardly here. This section of Sergief Island has been in private hands for many years. At some time or other all the trees that must have once stood on the small plateaus leading down to the cove were cut, probably for firewood. So around the house area have grown wild berry plants, Indian celery and grasses. When the warmth of June seeps into the ground the plants fairly explode into life. Without vigilance we'd find ourselves barely able to see out a window.

So, we embarked on a program of judiciously keeping growth in check. Jeff, while he was here, more than did his part: swinging scythes and machetes; maneuvering tillers, brush cutters and lawn mowers. We still don't have a polished, landscaped setting, but we have an area to enjoy, complete with flower beds, a grassy play area, trails bordered by native plants, and of course, our garden plots. It's been worth doing for several reasons. One is that it makes me feel better, perhaps a little more comfortable — the transplanted domesticated daisy, so to speak, among the lush wild growth. Another reason is that it offers us protection from the bugs. The mosquitos, stinging gnats, and deerflies are much fewer now. Keeping the vegetation cut destroys their habitation and makes living easier.

There were times in our first years when we felt intimidated about stepping out the door. To work at all it was necessary to burn smudge pots close to the area of activity. The need is sometimes still there but not nearly so often; it's possible now to enjoy a rest on the porch in the cool of an evening. But don't expect to come to summertime Alaska without receiving a few insect bites.

* * *

Power saws are a marvelous labor-saving device if you depend on getting wood to heat your home. The old crosscut saw my Dad used to pull was backbreaking and took much more time. We should, however, have one on hand. If it should become impossible, for any reason, to obtain fuel, the handsaw could be the means of keeping us warm and fed.

Lloyd likes the Stihl brand of power saw. Lee likes any that will give him reasonably trouble-free service, since he's usually the one putting it to use. Anyone making much use of a power saw must learn to keep it in general repair and, certainly, learn to sharpen the chain. A dull chain gives you slow, angled cuts and much more wear and tear on your machine. A guide that makes sharpening relatively simple is available to clamp on the bar. The silt that blows down from the river during parts of the year settles on the trees, giving them a gritty crust that makes chain sharpening a regular necessity.

When I first began this book I intended to include a chapter on hunting and the guns necessary to bring in the game. I've since decided to leave that subject for people much more knowledgeable than I. Numerous books and publications wait to instruct the hunter — expert or novice.

Enough for me to say that guns, bullets and reloading equipment are part of the tools of our trade of self-sufficiency. People here, I believe, view hunting as a means to live. We kill only to eat, and no animal on Sergief Island or the surrounding area dies wantonly or is wasted by us.

There seems no end to the kinds of firearms available; each hunter has his own preferences and prejudices. Lloyd likes automatics, Lee and Jeff prefer bolt action. I don't have a rifle, although I like to shoot. I intend, one day, to get something a little smaller than a 7mm, but at any rate, the 7mm magnum rifles the men here own make the kill swift and clean. A chain saw and winch help in handling game, and good-quality sharp knives are something you must have.

Once we get our game home and it's hung the required time of one to two weeks, depending on the temperature, we cut it up ourselves using an assembly-line procedure of sawing, cutting, grinding and double wrapping. For grinding we use a large Universal Meat Chopper #333, which does the job fast and efficiently.

I mix some of the ground meat with sausage seasoning, making a very acceptable breakfast patty. I have a sausage stuffer and packaged casings, but for some unfathomable reason have never gotten around to using them. One sausage seasoning I'm especially fond of is Legg's Old Plantation Pork Sausage Seasoning. A little goes a long way and it's very good. Or, it's easy to simply add thyme, sage, garlic, onion powder, and salt and pepper to create your own mix. It's best to season a small amount, keeping track of the proportions, then fry a little to test until you get it to your liking. There are many brands of prepared seasonings on the market — easily found.

* * *

I probably don't need to mention that a good supply of wrenches and hammers, a level, plumb line, nails of various sizes, all sizes of nuts and bolts, wire, handsaws, shovels, rakes, post-hole digger, and things I can't think of right now all make remote living tolerable. You'll find yourself doing, repairing, and building things you never anticipated, and the more you have on hand to do the job the more pleasure you'll find in meeting the challenge. Keep an open eye and mind, too, about using things in ways for which they were never intended. Use that creativity! Each wilderness dweller has to decide for himself, after considerable thought, which tools he *must* have and which are just nice to have. There is a difference, and if you wait until you have all of the worthwhile possibilities you'll probably never move.

As I write this chapter there's a challenge I'm not meeting. It's my own fault, too. I'm alone on the island, and will be for a few weeks. Lloyd and Lee have gone south; Jeff and Sethnie are working in Wrangell.

My problem is that I've never learned to adequately understand our electrical system. Yesterday, I somehow managed to knock loose the lead to the house from our bank of batteries and can't seem to find the right connection to restore power to the radio and CB. I think I've tried every possible connection but nothing works. Woe is me. It goes to prove that each member of a remote community should understand and know how to operate all the vital equipment. I've always resisted mechanical things, so now here I sit with my thin line to civilization broken.

Well, maybe there'll be some boats going up-river when the tide starts in and I can flag some Good Samaritan who knows more about these things than I.

I feel a little ashamed that I'm not able to handle a problem as relatively simple as the one facing me. This time alone on the island will probably do me good in forcing me to use and understand more of the tools that are necessary here.

There's a hummingbird coming repeatedly to the window this morning, checking out the delphiniums and disappointed, I believe, in finding the buds still closed. He'll have to take his sharp little tool of a beak over to the columbine. They're waving at him, in full bloom.

You see, if you can't do it one way, you do it another. The most powerful tool any of us can own is the desire and determination of our own spirit to make things go — somehow — and do it with good cheer.

Wood from the far beach arrives via barge, with Sethnie and Jeff aboard.

VI
FINDING WAYS TO PINCH A PENNY

When we came to Alaska in 1979 we felt we were reasonably well prepared to take care of our own material needs and even to help those who might follow us establish themselves. We had assets and investments that, combined with Alaskan money-making projects, we believed would sustain us . . . but we failed to reckon with the oncoming recession. The value of some of those assets plummeted; the value of timber on the island, valued at $400 per board foot at time of purchase, fell to around $150. It was a rude shock to our plans, postponing many of them and initiating a lot of money-saving or money-making techniques that might not before have been necessary.

I'm no stranger to thrift. As a child I experienced the rigors of the Depression, not being rescued from it until World War II made every man (or woman) valuable if they could weld or operate a riveting gun, and I was able to share in the swell of activity.

Although I consider myself a thrifty woman, my husband doesn't share in that evaluation. He frequently refers me back to how his grandmother could stretch a dollar, commenting on how I always spend "to the wire." Well, maybe. I'm not convinced. Our years here have quelled my acquisitive instincts — or is it just lack of temptation, by not having all the luscious malls to cruise?

If I have a taste for caviar I've been able to admirably restrain it. My tastes run to thick tweeds, translucent china, and furniture first familiar to Louis XIV (I'd settle for a good copy), but none of these items overrun the cabin on Sergief Island. That doesn't imply, however, that there's any real lack here.

Anyone moving to a self-sustaining life style must learn to simplify their yearnings, or they merely change abode.

One cardinal rule is not to buy junk. That isn't as easy as it sounds, as we learned in several instances. It isn't always easy to know whether an item is good quality or not. Price, often, is not the determiner. With tools, parts, and mechanical equipment the testimony of current users is probably as good an assurance as you can get. Even good-quality merchandise is a waste of money if it isn't precisely what you need. The down jacket may be a great and durable piece of clothing, but it is a poor choice if you have to try to warm yourself beneath its sodden feathers during a year drenched by eighty inches of rainfall. A V-hull boat may be a great buy, with lots of stability in the water, but it's not for you if you have to maneuver it over the shallow waters of the Stikine Flats or try to keep it from being on its side on the beach when the river is low and the tide is out.

So, how do we go about making do with what we have? If I say one way is to take care of what we already have, you'll have to promise not to laugh if you examine the carcasses of discarded boats adorning the cove. You might be tempted to say we aren't practicing what I preach, but it's still a good rule.

Many's the time I've put to use an item of clothing nobody's worn for five years, or made a patchwork gift or doll's dress from scraps of cloth I've accumulated over the years. Hauled them up here, too. The yarn I bought ten years ago for fifty cents a skein sells for about two dollars now, so don't smile too broadly at my little investments. (I haven't figured how much it cost me to get it up here.)

I've always been handy with the hair shears, and if my customers have a way of dwindling as they reach a certain age, I don't take it personally or let it cast a shadow on my expertise. The first time Doug took a look in the mirror and decided I didn't give his coiffure *quite* the look he was after, I said, "Well, fine. You'll just have to patronize the barber of your choice." When Jeff did the same thing a few years later it was humbling, but I bucked up under the blow. I still have two captive customers, Lloyd and Lee, who want fairly conventional haircuts. It works out fine, if I'm careful to cut their hair a few days before a trip to town so the rough spots have a chance to blend. Sethnie usually wears her hair long — thank goodness — but she sometimes condescends to have me cut her bangs if she thinks her allowance is too short to pay the fourteen dollars charged locally. I've cut my own hair but I honestly don't recommend it. It makes for bad posture as you try to pull your head into your collar bone.

All kidding aside, we've saved a lot of money through my hair-cutting and it hasn't induced any permanent traumas.

I used to be a great advocate of home permanents, too, but my ideas have changed. I don't know whether my hair is different or the permanent formulas have changed, but the end result is a far cry from what it used to be. About the only benefit I get from them is that a set lasts longer.

So I have a solution. Along about March I begin a series of small economies, like giving each person one less egg occasionally and putting the value thereof in a jar, or claiming every stray piece of change around the house (I'll accept paper money, too). By the time June rolls around and I want to be presentable for the big Fourth of July bash in Wrangell, or we're hopefully getting ready to go south for camp meeting, I saunter into one of the local beauty shops, trying to avoid eye contact with the proprietor (after all, I haven't patronized her shop for a year). It doesn't work, though. She takes a look and says something like, "Oh, you're back for your yearly venture into the world of beauty." She does a great job anyway, and except for one trim in between it lasts me until the next go-round. After all, four of those months I'll spend ice-locked on the island, and my companions there don't seem to notice if my perm has grown out or not. My little expenditure at the beauty shop isn't exactly on my thrift list, but it's worth every penny to my overall well-being. I won't tell you how much it costs — my husband may read this book someday.

When I lived in Washington I took great delight in garage sales, rummage sales and every reasonable facsimile. Why not pay only a dollar for something that would cost many times that amount if purchased new? Some items, like pieces of china or bric-a-brac, become more valuable to the senses as you ponder the piece, wondering how many lives it has touched and what it meant to another person.

Clothes can be another matter. You don't really want someone to come up to you and say, "I had a shirt *just* like that. Hmm, it even had that little pucker on the left shoulder. I gave mine to the church rummage sale." That's never happened to me, but I've decided if it ever does I'll say, "Well, I was so happy to be able to help a charitable effort by making use of someone's old clothes." I probably won't ever have reason to say something like that and I probably wouldn't say it if I did. People are generally much too kind and tactful to ever put another human being in that position. But the thought does go through the minds of those who shop sometime or another in the marts of used clothing.

In the first place, any manufactured article is made in the multiple thousand, so the original owner/donor didn't own the only one in existence (especially if it doesn't have a pucker on the left shoulder). In the second place, so what if someone recognizes something they've given away? Maybe they liked it a lot and hated to part with it after they'd gained a pound too many. That's happened to me, and I'd have been happy to see that article of clothing being well used, going down the street on a trim body.

What this boils down to is that I know of few better ways to stretch a fixed amount of money than to shop for good used items. You may come up with a treasure. I'm not in Wrangell often enough to hit many garage sales, but the Salvation Army Thrift Store is usually open. There I can spend as long as I like going through piles of things folks have decided are no longer useful to them. Some of them are useful to me.

One of the many things my son-in-law, Bob, and I share is a love of garage sales. He likes Depression glass, books and other goodies; I like whatever I happen to see. (That can be a problem.) When I'm on a trip down south he knows he can always please me by saying, "Well, Mom, let's find some garage sales."

* * *

I've already covered some of the food economies I practice, but I didn't mention the soup jar. Leftover portions of vegetables, rice, noodles, or bits of meat, cut fine, go into a jar to make soup. When the jar gets full enough to make a batch, or old enough that it must be used promptly, it all goes into a pot along with a quart of stock I made during our last butchering. Whatever's in the jar determines what kind of soup it will be. Sometimes a creamed type, more often it turns into a minestrone with chopped canned tomatoes, finely sliced cabbage and some Italian spices. It may not be purist enough for the soup connoisseur but it tastes good to me. When it's simmered long on the back of the wood stove and you come in from long hours of outdoor work it can rival the cuisine of the gods, especially with a great slab of homemade bread.

* * *

There are lots of little economies everyone knows about but seldom practices anymore, like darning socks and underwear or putting an unobtrusive patch where it's needed. I understand that many of us have traded our time for the dollars that time will bring in the marketplace. Sometimes it's easier to buy a new pair of socks than find time to fix the old ones. I understand all that, but I question the soundness of the premise from which the conclusion is drawn. Time should not be continually nipping at our heels, and a system that requires it should be changed. That's what simpler living is all about. Of course you don't want to spend all those "free" hours darning socks. How about painting a picture or writing a poem?

I'm always on the watch for ways to use items that would ordinarily be thrown away. A real thrill of creativity floods my parsimonious soul as I find a new use for a plastic container, or even eggshells.

Did you know that the cooled water in which you've boiled your morning egg can give a real boost to your house plants; that the powdered shell can be a healthful mineral addition to your dog or cat menu; that eggshells are always good for your compost pile?

Compost is a way to see that no fruit or vegetable refuse is ever wasted. There are lots of good directions for making compost, but it need not be complicated. Simply layer all your scraps and clippings with thin layers of garden soil; keep the pile moist; and turn it every few days until the heating of decomposition stops and the results are a loose, fragrant product your plants will thank you for. If you don't feel like turning the pile to keep the air flowing it will take much longer to reach the desired stage, but it *will* eventually become compost.

I don't deny Sophie, the Newfoundland dog, the joy of gnawing on the bones she loves, but every so often I tour the yard, gathering all her old bones. They are tossed into the heater to be turned into bone meal. When we clean out the ashes they are mixed into the compost pile or saved in a dry container until I need them for a particular plant.

Some quick economies that I find useful are these: Save

your bacon grease; it adds flavor to many dishes where a little shortening is needed. Save the trimmed fat from beef for tying to trees for the birds. Save some of the styrofoam "peanuts" that come as packing protection — they provide great drainage for the bottoms of your house plant containers. Save some of the 2-liter soft drink bottles with black bottoms. Cut off evenly at any height, they make good small plant containers. Cut-down waxed milk cartons with drainage holes poked into the bottom make good containers in which to start seedlings.

When those cotton socks you don't want to darn start to pile up you can avoid feeling guilty by cutting spiraling strips from the top and using them as plant ties.

Plastic gallon containers have many second uses after appropriate cutting, ranging from funnels, scoops, plant protectors, and holders of plant food to buoys to mark the channel on the flats.

None of these uses are exclusive to Sergief Island. Many of them could better be practiced elsewhere. Making a dollar do double-duty is a state of mind, and it need not be burdensome. I've always viewed with aversion those with a tendency to follow me around turning out the lights. If an act of thrift is going to perform its function in pride it must be done unobtrusively, with care not to tarnish the luster of your life or the lives of those around you. So if you're going to substitute a tablespoon of water for one of the eggs in a recipe, keep your mouth shut. If you're patching a child's jeans for the third time make that patch colorful, in the shape of a kite, ball or butterfly, and do it with pride.

* * *

When we came here it wasn't our intention to retire. Lots of timber on our piece of the island should be salable. The timber also could provide work. Some of the young people involved with us in the move intended to become engaged in the fishing industry. This has become more difficult as several fisheries have come under the laws of limited entry. Fishing is not impossible, but it requires much more money than in the past. Gone are the days when any young person with a small boat could go out and hand-troll himself some kind of an income. This has proven to be a hardship to many who would like to enter the industry, particularly the young without financial backing. But, for better or worse, that's the way it is.

It was my hope and intention that others would live on the island and that one or more cottage industries would be developed. There is artistic talent among us and a good deal of determination. I've had lots of ideas. The fact that none of them have come to fruition hasn't dampened my enthusiasm . . . too much. I'd better not explain all my ideas in detail. After all, they might be valuable one of these days, so I'm keeping them under my hat.

When Jeff went to college I sent him off gladly, with the hope he would become a photojournalist. What better way to keep the island as his home base than to freelance around Alaska? Beautiful, fascinating Alaska has thousands of stories that have never been told, scenes that have never or rarely been pictured. After a couple of years he's changed direction, so I'm doubtful his activities will center on the island, but time will tell. I've picked up the writing torch — in a minor way — and if the torch gets heavy and my arm gets tired, I still have Sethnie coming along.

While Jeff lived here, he spent two winters trapping. He didn't get appreciably wealthier but he learned a lot. I did, too.

On December 14 of 1980 Jeff made his first catch, a small marten. The marten is a beautiful animal with glossy dark fur, big ears and feet. When Jeff brought it into the kitchen my first feeling was sadness, but I had to curb that thought. Jeff had spent many hours in frigid weather setting traps in which he'd invested most of his monetary assets. He was proud of the fact he'd succeeded and I wasn't going to dull it for him. He'd read and studied and gone out by himself when it would have been easier to sit by the fire.

That evening he rigged up a rod in the header of the doorway separating the kitchen and main room and strung up his marten. With his knife carefully sharpened, book with pictured directions on the drainboard, he started skinning. It wasn't quick but he did a good job and got considerably faster as the winter wore on. That was our first winter on the island; Lloyd was in Washington and I had many an anxious moment when Jeff failed to come back to the cabin by the time night fell. I thought of legs broken after going into a snow-covered hole, attacks by animals, and other things.

The island is not a particularly safe place in certain areas. The marsh flats are safest when solidly frozen, but high tides that wash over the flats can catch you, cutting off your access to higher ground if you're unwary. When the ice is rotting it's easy to miscalculate its strength and fall through into one of the deep, icy sloughs that intersect the marsh portion of the island. The higher, wooded areas are cut by deep ravines, hard to traverse in the daylight, impossible in the dark. Game trails take you over some hard terrain in unlikely places. The north end of the island has no beach for several thousand feet, only huge rocks that can be gotten over easily enough when the river is low, but only at great risk when the river is high but not frozen. All these things gave me pause to think. But a mother can't move her son to a wilderness area and then put fear into him by her constant admonitions.

So, Jeff learned orienteering; I grew confident he would always know where he was, and that he would exercise reasonable caution. While trapping would not be my first choice of a way to make a living, I am not burdened by a sense of guilt about it. I know it is no more inhumane than many of the ways in which domestic animals are brought to market. One doesn't necessarily justify the other, of course, but at least the trapped animal killed by a quick clip to the back of the head isn't suffering in the same degree as the chicken doomed to spend her entire life in a cage barely big enough to allow her to turn around, or the pig forced to farrow in a pen too small to allow her to reach her young, or milk cows never allowed to get off the blacktop smothering the green land that is their heritage.

Now you know why I want an old-time self-sustaining farm, not geared to squeeze the last cent out of pitiable animals to pay ever-higher interest to moneylenders.

In addition to his stack of marten hides Jeff caught a wolf the first winter; that pleased him. Early in February he went out in the afternoon to check his traps. He checked them regularly and the chore had become so routine to him he left without a gun. Very unwise. Just before sunset he came running in, winded and very excited. A wolf was caught in a marten trap just behind the old barn. None of us could understand why the small trap held the creature, but hoping it would still be there when he got back, Jeff grabbed his .22; Lee followed him with a larger rifle. The wolf was still there and they carried it home stretched between them on a 2 by 4. It was a large female with a beautiful pelt that measured seventy-two by fifty-eight inches. It was held by the small marten trap because its legs had been previously injured, preventing it from getting a good pull.

It wasn't the only wolf Jeff trapped that winter. On the other end of the island, by a downed moose carcass, he made a regular wolf set. Skillfully too, evidently, because the wolf is one of the most wily of animals. When he checked the set he found he'd caught the one that got away. His stakes were pulled; the trap showed evidence of having held a wolf . . . for a while.

I hear a wolf howl occasionally, and feel a sympathy for the creature who, over the long snow-covered months, must kill to eat. I long for that day when "The wolf and the lamb shall feed together" . . . and "They shall not hurt nor destroy in all my holy mountain."

The next winter Jeff left the confines of the island, walking the frozen reaches of the Stikine. He spent nights in cabins miles from home, once having to stay in an unheated cabin in minus 15°(F) weather. His down sleeping bag proved its worth that night. When I saw him coming down the river the next day in a howling wind, icicles hanging from the nose piece of his face mask, I gave thanks for his safe return.

Such are the lengths one goes to save and make a dollar in the wilderness.

Anchored in a cove, the Carver *is within wading distance for Sethnie.*

VII
WATER TRAVEL

Living on an island sounds so great; and it is. Living on an island conjures up mind pictures of charming small boats traveling over sparkling smooth waters to coves beautifully fitted out with docks, ramps and easy moorings. It can be that way.

Living on a small island in Southeast Alaska usually means isolation, not only from other human beings but from cars, roads, stores — most things that twentieth-century Americans take for granted — as well as from the stimulating activities of organized churches, night classes, city council meetings, and even the convivial glass at the local pub, if that be your bent.

The fact that you're also isolated from crime, pollution, and local property taxes is only partially consoling when you're struck by the whim-whams of boredom or loneliness.

The romance of living on an island in a wilderness area strikes deep chords in the hearts of those who have long planned such a move — or read enough wilderness books. The fact that we knew little or nothing about water transportation and boats did nothing to dampen our enthusiasm. We could drive a car, couldn't we? What could be so different about boats?

Well, I for one cannot tell you all the differences between cars and boats, but there are a few striking ones that come much too clearly to mind. One is that if you're in a car and you run out of gas or your motor quits you can pull over to the side of the road, raise your hood, and either fix the problem or wait for the help of a passing motorist. In a boat, you'd better be prepared to get running before the tide throws you onto some rocks, sweeps you out to sea, or goes out from under you, leaving you high and dry on a sand bar for the next six hours.

A second small example is that unless you've managed to find yourself driving in the middle of an earthquake, the road doesn't usually come up to meet you, toss you about, or disappear from in front of you. The waters of the Stikine flats are guilty of all these capricious acts.

I can see the Wrangell Airport from our front window. The town itself is around a bend of Wrangell Island, shielded from view. It's only about eight miles from here to the safety of the harbor in town. You'd think that fairly intelligent people could manage to negotiate those few miles in reasonable safety. Wouldn't you?

After Lloyd contracted to buy the island property, he set about shopping for a boat. He'd been told by local people about many of the pitfalls connected with traversing the waters between Sergief Island and Wrangell: the sometimes-fierce winds and turbulent waters of the back channel; the shallow waters of the river estuary that make a close watch on tide heights essential; strong, frigid winds out of the river basin in spring and late fall; and icebergs and submerged snags — all to be watched for and given consideration.

Lloyd found a tough 24-foot glassed plywood, dory-hull riverboat. It had a 455 Oldsmobile motor with a Berkley jet outdrive. With the often-shallow waters we had to travel, the jet seemed like a good idea. It could propel the flat-bottomed boat in waters of less than a foot. Nobody mentioned that the silty waters of the Stikine are death on jets, or that slush ice, frequent in early winter, has the nasty habit of clogging the jet. It would have been nice if they had — before we bought a boat. Several folks mentioned these facts later.

So, we bought the *Red Eye* and hauled it up here; that chore wasn't without its peculiar tribulations. We almost lost the boat to fire before we got out of Seattle. The long-unused trailer that came with the boat had an ungreased wheel that heated until it burst into flame on an overpass on the outskirts of the city. By the time passers-by made us aware of the problem (we were driving the moving van, which limited our vision), the tire was on fire, sending flames up the side of the boat. We had one fire extinguisher that was wasted by a too-helpful person who grabbed it from Lloyd's hands and directed the chemical at the flame itself instead of its source. I lost my coat and burned my arm trying to smother the flames. I believe we might have lost the boat then and there except for a motorist who stopped and put his large fire extinguisher to work in exactly the proper manner. We'll always be grateful to him, but in the confusion, he left before we could even tell him, "Thank you."

In British Columbia the trailer broke loose from the van, sending the *Red Eye* over snowbanks into a deep ditch where she was eventually rescued by a road crew.

When we finally loaded the *Red Eye* and ourselves onto the ferry, *Taku*, in Prince Rupert, it was with great relief. The tension had been no small thing, but we didn't know the adventures of the *Red Eye* were far from over.

We didn't use it much that first winter because, as I've already explained, it was too late in the year for us to move onto the island. We ran it long enough, however, to find a few things wrong. It nickeled and dimed us to death — not all defects in the *Red Eye*, but expenses for rope, anchors, buoys, fire extinguishers, extra water hoses, and sundries large and small.

Then we learned the boat wouldn't plane, if it carried any appreciable weight, without running the motor wide open; even then planing wasn't a sure thing. Now, planing means the boat is lifted partially onto the surface of the water by the churning revolutions of its propeller or jet drive. If the boat won't plane you're reduced to hull speed, which is the speed the particular hull can be pushed through the water. After it reaches its speed, more power makes only a very small difference.

Running a motor at full speed is a bad idea. Boat motors, except for diesel, are notoriously short-lived, and running at excessively high rpms can reduce that life considerably. So we decided, on the advice of people in the business, to try a reduction gear that we hoped would turn the jet at high speeds while allowing the motor to run at a slower rate. We sent for the gear. It cost $1,000 plus freight — and it didn't work.

We went back to the original drive system, and resigned ourselves to some slow trips the next spring as we moved our belongings to the island.

Before leaving Washington we'd built a barge on which to transport our things over the flats. It measures 18 by eight feet by four feet high. It has a double bottom, giving it good buoyancy while also giving it the appearance of being top-heavy. But in spite of going through some very rough waters, the barge has never up-ended or lost its cargo.

It did make a comical picture, loaded high with boxes, furniture, tools, appliances, and people. When we got around to transporting my old oak table and the piano, I was thankful for that four feet of height. As we'd leave Wrangell harbor, stuff tied down, kids riding on top (on a davenport if that happened to be the load of the day), we saw many a smile and a raised eyebrow. Sometimes the crew on incoming boats would indicate by hand signal the condition of the water we could expect to encounter. I think that June had more rough water than any summer month since. Twice we were forced to turn around and make our way back to Wrangell, there to unload or try to carefully cover the day's freight, depending on what it was. When we finally made the last barge trip and hand-carried the last items up the bank we had cause for celebrating. Oh, for the decadent bourgeois tools of the Industrial Revolution — like a tractor.

The barge hasn't made many trips to town since that first summer — only a time or two to haul a winter's supply of fuel and propane. It sits on the beach, waiting to make the return trip, heaven forbid, when one or another of us decides our mantle of loneliness lies too heavily.

We didn't really have to worry about the *Red Eye* very long. We lost it the second winter on the last trip from town.

On December 7, 1981, all of us except Jeff went to town, thinking we had a last chance to get some Christmas gifts and other provisions. The weather was mild, barely freezing, with only a small amount of scum ice on the beach. High tide was about 4:30 P.M., so to give us time to complete our business we decided to stay over one night and start back as early as possible the next day, to avoid being caught out after dark. At that time of year daylight is down to between six and seven hours, which meant we had to try to reach home two or more hours before the high tide of the following day. During the fall and early winter months, when there are usually winds and many extremely high tides, it's a good idea to travel as soon as there's water enough after low tide to escape the rush of water accompanying the highs.

We left Wrangell about 2:30 P.M. It was a bit rough in the back channel (the channel that cuts up the back of Wrangell Island and the mainland), but it didn't cause us concern. We got very near Sergief Island when we began to run into slush ice, tiny bits of ice almost like ice cubes run through a blender. It was several inches thick; the weather had become markedly colder overnight. When we'd talked to Jeff on the CB he'd acknowledged the ice had thickened, but since it was loose he didn't think we'd have any problem getting through it.

Suddenly the power failed — the jet-drive was filled with ice. A wind of around fifty miles per hour had struck us when we reached the river's influence; ice was building on the chain and hull of the boat.

Lee fought his way out onto the bow to drop an anchor, as we were being swept rapidly downstream. The men cleaned out the jet and got the motor running once, twice, three times, only to have it immediately plug again. We were so close to home! At one time ten minutes would have seen us into the cove.

It seemed the only solution was to get Jeff to come out in the small aluminum skiff to tow us in. I was frightened for us in the *Red Eye*, but even more for Jeff. It was bitterly cold, the wind chill factor must have been well below zero, the motor on the skiff wasn't all that reliable, and he was still a boy.

My thoughts went to Sethnie, too. Her small, thirteen-year-old face was pinched; worried eyes searched mine in the gathering dusk. Putting my arms around her, we huddled in the cabin waiting to hear the drone of the motor that would mean Jeff was approaching. I tried to assure her, and myself, that God surely hadn't allowed us to come to our island home only to let us drown on the flats.

There it was. He was coming. But it didn't sound right; he was coming slowly, as if he lacked power. It turned out the controls were frozen, and he couldn't fight them open.

Trying to attach a tow rope from one boat to another in turbulent seas, freezing rain, in the dark, with strong winds is an exercise in courage and tenacity, with some good fortune thrown in — if you're able to pull it off. They got the boats tied together, and Jeff opened the small Johnson motor on the skiff as far as it would go, aiming for the cove that by this time was somewhat upstream and across the main channel of current.

It was no good. We made no progress. The swift current, strong winds and limited power all worked against us. There was nothing to do but allow ourselves to be carried somewhat downstream and try to angle across the current enough to hit the lower end of the island. By this time several hours had elapsed and the tide was on its way out. There was no time to lose if we hoped to reach the shelter of home that night.

Jeff started towing in that direction and, aided by the wind and current, progress was rapid; but as he attempted to make for shore the *Red Eye* drove itself into a barely submerged sand bar. There was no budging it.

We knew there was no hope of moving it until the next tide came in, and since we were now very cold, some of us wet, it seemed sensible to anchor the boat, leave it until tomorrow and then try to get it home. I had no real thought of the boat being in great danger.

We could step out of the boat onto gravel, walk to the edge of the bar and get into the skiff. We carried as much of our cargo as we could comfortably handle and started out. Even that short ride wasn't without its moments of fear, but as we edged into the cove I gave a prayer of thanksgiving.

The next morning the ice had piled up. The speed with which that can happen in this country is incredible. When conditions of wind and temperature are right you can go to bed with open water and get up to a beach covered with heavy ice.

We could see that the anchor on the *Red Eye* had dragged, but the riverboat was still relatively close, so if the weather gave a thawing trend we could get to it with the skiff; if it froze solid we could walk over the ice to get our things. It seemed that as long as the boat was in solid ice it would stay put.

Expecting the weather to warm, we tried to keep the thin ice of the cove broken up, to enable us to get the small boat out as soon as possible. After a stressful day we went to bed, leaving the skiff farther out in the cove than we would have ordinarily done, not wanting it to get encased in the ice of the beach.

The weather did warm. When we got up the next morning we saw that it had warmed enough to bring an avalanche of ice from up-river crashing down on us. As we watched, helpless, the eighteen-foot tide came in, throwing great icebergs about; ice cut the line on the skiff and took the *Red Eye*, still in its ice casing, off the bar and out to sea.

I didn't believe it. It was almost like standing impotently watching a friend die; a thing beyond understanding. There was nothing anyone could have done to help us as long as the boats were in that amount of ice. We followed them with the field glasses for as long as we could, bleeding a little inside. We weren't prepared to sustain a financial loss of that magnitude. We were also left without any type of transportation. Not that we needed transportation for a few months, but spring would come. At last look both boats were heading west, past High Island.

We of course got on the CB to Wrangell, asking people there to alert the Coast Guard, the local fishing services, and any boats in the area to be on the lookout. We still had hope that if the boats made it safely into salt water someone would be able to rescue them.

Many people tried to help. The word was out, and lots of folks watched. Days went by until, about ten days later, the *Red Eye* was spotted many miles from home, tossed up into, ironically, Quiet Harbor. The green aluminum skiff was never sighted. Presumably it swamped and is lying, somewhere, in deep water, home to barnacles and halibut. If someone in a far corner of Southeast Alaska happened to find it, I hope it was someone who needed it as badly as we did.

A man in Wrangell towed the *Red Eye* into town where it sat until spring, broken and dejected, its salt-soaked motor disintegrating in the rains and snows of winter. Of the several hundred dollars worth of groceries that had been on the boat, only a package of cheese and a soggy container of peppercorns remained.

That winter, for me, was one of discontent. As the wind blew and the snow piled to five feet I lay at night in our small attic, waking periodically as if from a nightmare, but the fear wasn't a dream. It was very real — the boats were gone. I brought up for question everything we'd done, including coming here in the first place. The coming of spring brought an easing of tensions, but a crack had opened in our container of faith and the healing left a weakness in the structure of the dream.

That spring of '82 Lloyd hitched a ride with a boat heading to Wrangell, carrying with him a small satchel and all the cash we could scrape together — money that was badly needed for other things. He shopped in Wrangell and Ketchikan, then took the ferry to Seattle to look for a boat.

He found a 23-foot wood-hull Carver. It had been a good boat at one time and had received considerable reconstruction. It had a completely rebuilt 302 Ford V8 engine with a Volvo outdrive. The V hull gave us a smoother ride, but it also required deeper water in which to travel. It was a good value, but I never liked it. We looked at that wood hull and found places where it was unsound, and when it slapped the water in heavy seas I expected to find the hull cracking under me. I began to be resentful of the fact that one emergency after another always seemed to take the money that should have gone into an auxiliary, kicker motor that would give us considerably more safety, and might have averted altogether the tragic loss of the first boats.

We bought another small aluminum skiff, in no way as good as the one we'd lost, equipped with a motor that made one trip across the flats before the lower unit went out.

In 1984 we bought a tough 21-foot glass dory hull. It was built for the Snake River and is a good sound boat, but its flat bottom gives a rough ride. Lloyd took the engine out of the Carver, putting it into the glass Hy-N-Dry. It should give us a few good years of use. As I write, Lloyd and Lee are working to put it into top condition for this year's use.

The idea that you can get by with a cheap boat as you might a cheap car, especially if you have to depend on it for transportation under conditions less than ideal, is just not so. We've had a lot of bad experiences on the water since coming here. Many of them were caused by inexperience and ignorance, some by just plain bad luck, but whichever, they were painful — and dangerous. If we had bought a tough aluminum-hull boat when we first came here, we would have been money ahead and certainly ahead in our enjoyment of the water around us. I look forward to the day when we'll be able to buy one, but then I'm an optimist. However, we finally bought a kicker.

Our experiences with the water have certainly not been all bad. A day exploring the channels and sloughs around us can be one of pure joy. There's a song that says the bluest skies are in Seattle. I'd argue that. The bluest, most beautiful skies I've seen are stretched over the shining fjordlike waters and green mountains of Southeast Alaska on a clear day. Nothing is finer than to pile into a boat with your lunch and a fishing pole.

Up the Stikine, another world waits as you visit the hot

tubs where the Forest Service has built attractive buildings to enclose the tubs and make your soaking in the mineral-rich waters enjoyable. Each slough seems vastly different in its scenic beauty. As you edge your boat along into the Twin Lake channel, the area seems almost tropical in its lush growth. If it weren't for the snow-capped mountains in the not-far distance, one could almost be persuaded he had been transported to the bayous of a southern state.

Even violent storms have their beauty in might and power, if you can enjoy them from a position of safety.

Many lives have been lost in the river, and on the flats between here and Wrangell. The area deserves respect, not fear. Whatever a person's surroundings, there are things to be learned, skills that help ensure survival. If there is more knowledge necessary here than in some other places, that is as it should be. Any other way and it would no longer be wilderness.

With all honesty, I can say that despite the painful lessons it's great to live on an island.

Sethnie enjoys one of the advantages of correspondence study.

VIII

COMMUNICATION AND EDUCATION

Communication is defined in the dictionary as a system of sending and receiving messages. To the folks of Sergief Island the best and most favored way of getting a message to someone is to hop into the boat and go tell them. When that isn't possible the CB comes in mighty handy.

It does have its drawbacks. Sometimes a jiving voice from Red Bluff, Tulsa, or Winnemucca will break in on you, a voice out of the air, a disengaged spirit to whom you can never communicate your need or share your cry to humanity from your little spot of the earth.

We usually are heard pretty well in Wrangell, however. Since Sethnie's been boarding and going to school in town, I wait for the call, "Sergief Island, are you by?" Her young voice sounds sweet and clear as I hurry to pick up the microphone. "Come in, Wildflower. This is Joy-bells." It's the highlight of my day, especially during the mini-days and maxi-nights of winter. So she tells me what she's learned that day in World History; how she barely squeaked by in an Algebra test; or that she expects to do well on her last report for English Composition III. There are lots of things that can't be told on the CB, like which boy has the most absolutely fantastic smile, or how stung she felt when another boy — the creep — failed to ask her to dance after the basketball tourney. It doesn't do to repeat too often, "I miss you." "I love you." But those are my feelings, and I can be thankful for the chance a CB gives me to hear a loved voice.

It also helps in many other ways: when your boat motor is down and you desperately need a part to be brought to you by some Good Samaritan in town; when you're broken down on the flats with the tide going out; or when you see from the cabin another boat in trouble and need to alert someone in town. It's comforting to know that if you have a serious accident you can call for help on the CB. While we've never had to use the CB in such an emergency, its availability is an insurance I appreciate.

When Jeff was up-river on his trap line in sub-zero weather it was worth a lot to be able to hear his answers to our questions — one click for yes, two for no. The little portable CB he carried wouldn't transmit his voice (although at two hundred dollars it should have) but those clicks told us he was okay.

During the winters on the river there is usually a trapper or two up in a lonely cabin, making his solitary way over remote windswept stretches of the river, sometimes crossing on rotting ice. We're glad to be a link in the trappers' chain of communication with folks who hold them in their hearts.

The first winter we were here Jeff relayed messages from two trappers up-river to their families on Zerembo Island. It enlivened the winter for him, putting him in touch with the lives of others in remote places. He and a fellow on another island even managed a game or two of Monopoly and Battleship, although this sort of thing is frowned upon by the FCC.

Because of the difficulty in maintaining CB contact, most fishing boats and many remote dwellers have gone to the use of VHF. We don't have one although it's in our future plans. With a VHF I could hook up to the radio phone and talk to folks anywhere I wanted. There I go again — bringing technology (and expense) to the wilderness — when I said I wanted a simpler way of life.

* * *

Are you a letter writer? I never was. I can remember my mother pointedly enclosing stamped envelopes and postcards in her letters to me. It seemed such an effort to sit down and try to make the small happenings of my life interesting to another person.

Living on Sergief Island has changed that for me. To get a letter is pure joy, and writing one has simply become another way of reaching out to another human who probably likes to get letters too. Age may have something to do with it.

It's become increasingly important to me to contact relatives and old friends who haven't been seen for years.

I write, also, to some whom I've never met except by letter; some are in prisons with bars, some in prisons of age or illness, but all have become friends, important to me in a very real way. And if a letter from an island in Alaska can make a life a little brighter then it's a valuable method of communication.

When I make it into town and find the large mailbox stuffed with mail it's enough to keep me busy for a long time — not that I have any trouble keeping busy. It's just that the good old U.S. Mail is still a fine means of communicating.

* * *

Another type of communication vital to many bush dwellers is the correspondence school. It would be hard for me to overstate my feelings of gratitude and enthusiasm for the treatment we received from both the Centralized Correspondence Study Center in Juneau and the Southeast Island School District in Ketchikan.

Looking back now, with Jeff across the miles at college and Sethnie boarding in Wrangell, the years they spent working on their studies here in the small cabin on Sergief Island seem incredibly precious to me. It seems Jeff's head should still be bent over the desk, contemplating the intricacies of English grammar; or Sethnie should be sitting at the table, her pastels and pencils spread before her as she strives to capture the essence of the picture propped before her. My cry is only that of so many parents through time, "Where did the time go?" Did I simply allow it to slide like oil through my fingers, leaving only a residue of memory, or was it stolen when I, in an unwary moment, glanced away in too long a look at my pots, pans, and petty grievances?

We weren't entirely unfamiliar with correspondence education when we arrived in Alaska. In January of 1977 Lloyd and I embarked on an evangelistic tour of several states that necessitated taking Jeff and Sethnie out of their local school. We enrolled the kids in a private, religious correspondence course for that semester.

We had a good-sized fifth-wheel trailer pulled by a four-door pick-up, so we were comfortable and they had adequate room to study. Mornings and some evenings were usually devoted to study, as we interspersed our church appointments with parks and local sights along the way. They did their lessons to the tune of a waterfall at Yosemite, the call of a hawk over the Grand Canyon, or to the strain of the opening song at a church service. It was a fun trip. If the kids lacked a bit in some subjects, they learned a lot about geography, natural history, and the face of America, expressed in both the natural beauty around them and the faces of their fellow men.

We didn't think much of that particular correspondence course. Other than the books and lesson outlines, the kids received little specific instruction. Their lessons were never returned to them so they could see their errors, and we thought the emphasis was heavy on one particular political viewpoint. Anyway, it got them through the year and that fall they were back in public school.

Before you embark on a home school program you should make inquiries about the laws governing home study in your particular state. There are ways to accomplish your purpose, if you're tenacious, but the school authorities in many states take a dim view of the whole process. Parents have even been jailed, their children placed in foster care. So be sure you are legally sound in what you attempt in this line. All conscientious parents want their children to be well educated, able to take their place in the world with dignity and awareness; most educational authorities do too. The friction comes from the differing viewpoints on how best to bring about that end.

We had heard that Alaska had a state-operated correspondence system for remote families and as an alternative educational option for folks in town, so shortly after our arrival here late in 1979 we started making inquiries.

We made a call to the Centralized Correspondence Study Center in Juneau, and back came applications and catalogs. For Sethnie, in the sixth grade, the choices were more structured and limited, but for Jeff, then a junior, the choice of courses available to him was wide and the resources offered us generous.

In a few weeks the Post Office handed us boxes of materials, all in extremely good shape or new, accompanied by pencils, paper, pens — everything needed for any particular course, including art materials and P.E. equipment. It was fun to open the boxes and see all the good things to work with.

At Central in Juneau is a staff of teachers who prepare and grade most of the subjects for grade school students and many of the courses of high school kids. The balance, those courses that have not yet been prepared by our own teachers, are purchased from the University of Nebraska correspondence system, or from American School in Chicago. For these courses the student sends his lessons to the respective school, where they are graded, then they are sent back through the student's counselor in Juneau and on to the student himself.

We grew to especially appreciate the subjects handled directly through Juneau. You get to feel comfortable with a particular teacher and are encouraged to call any of them when necessary (when you can get near a phone). They have great understanding of the remote student, offering special-project equipment as they can. They made it possible for Jeff to participate in a work experience in Juneau, which, at his choice, was in the field of journalism. His board, transportation and expenses were paid, right down to pocket money. Interest was shown in him that he still remembers and appreciates.

In the spring of 1981, Jeff received notice that he'd been chosen as one of the two students sponsored by Centralized Correspondence Study to attend the Close Up program in Washington, D.C. In conjunction with the trip he was required to complete a course of study on government and write a report on his experiences for the school paper when he returned (yes, they have a school paper). He started working with gusto, and before I knew it there was a floatplane out in the cove waiting to pick him up and transport him to the jet in Wrangell.

He had a happy, busy time, learning about government, associating with other young people, and seeing our nation. It was an experience he might never have had if he hadn't been a "Bush kid."

Sethnie also was chosen for a special experience when she was selected to attend the Fine Arts Camp in Sitka. This is conducted on the campus of Sheldon Jackson College in Sitka. The offerings include all sorts of voice and instrumental music, dance and theater arts. She appreciated being able to go, but it was one of her first experiences away from her family so was hard on her. This, too, was on a scholarship basis — all expenses paid. One of her teachers in Juneau even met her and arranged for her to room with her daughter.

I understand that shyness and aversion to new situations is one of the disadvantages suffered by young people coming out of remote villages and other isolated spots all over Alaska. It requires real courage to meet whole groups of new people and adjust to unfamiliar customs and circumstances. Sethnie had a natural tendency to shyness and in that way island living didn't help her. Experiences in later years have helped; living in Wrangell has opened social opportunities for her. I hope and believe she's learned that she's a lovely young person who has qualities and insights others can recognize and appreciate.

Correspondence study is not all fun and games. The materials sent are thorough and sometimes exhaustive. When all information must be imparted by way of the printed page, rather than a classroom situation with lectures and demonstrations, it makes for a great deal of reading — sometimes bringing on boredom and lethargy.

There is often a problem finding a place where your student can study without distraction. It isn't always easy to obtain cooperation from other family members — to convince them that some activity of theirs should be curtailed until school time is over, or that they don't really have to hear a certain radio program. Larger quarters would certainly have made the whole thing easier.

It's important, too, for the student to have someone to bounce their thoughts and ideas upon. It's also important to break up the studying with physical activity. In the case of a younger child, of course, it takes a great deal of time on the part of the mother or other home instructor to teach, explain and keep the child interested. There's a tendency for the child to spend more and more time on his studies until he (and Mom) finds himself with little or no free time and always behind on his work. It's important to set deadlines for a certain segment of the work to be done and see that the deadline is met.

I've seen both Jeff and Sethnie sitting at their work, eyes glazed, thoughts miles away, until a question or comment from me brought them back to the task at hand. It isn't always easy, and anyone contemplating correspondence study should be ready to encounter the problems. But, the advantages can also be very real.

There's a freedom seldom experienced any other way. When the work is done your time is your own, wherever you are. The values imparted to your children during the most critical years of their lives are, for the most part, your own. Academically, I don't think either of the children suffered. Jeff carries a grade point of around 3.5 in college, and Sethnie is doing fine in high school. I'm not underestimating the value of a good teacher. A good one is of inestimable value in stimulating interest in an inquiring mind; and a teacher I'm not. There are schools where Jeff and Sethnie might have received more thorough, richer learning experiences, but many where they would have received considerably less.

On discussing the whole correspondence experience with Jeff recently, I asked him how he thought it had affected his work in college. He told me that, overall, he felt he arrived at school as well (or better) equipped as his fellow freshmen.

There were some notable blank spots on his education, chiefly in mathematics and chemistry. That wasn't necessarily the fault of the correspondence system — the courses were available. Those weren't fields, however, that either Lloyd or I were equipped to help him in, so Jeff has had to work very hard to pick up these subjects. Of course, I never expected him to major in the sciences, and he'll graduate next year with a B.S. in biology. I'm very proud of what he's been able to accomplish and I think correspondence played its part in teaching him that it's basically up to us what we learn.

The years were, for me, something I'd never exchange for anything anyone could offer in trade. In those days we'd say, "Well, get that subject done and we'll take off for the flats." So a head bowed over a book would rise, eyes light, and soon we'd be on our way, sandwiches in our pockets, the dogs at our heels.

> The heart is the capital of the Mind,
> The Mind is a single State.
> The Heart and the Mind together make
> A single continent.
>
> One — is the population —
> Numerous enough.
> This ecstatic nation
> Seek — it is Yourself.
>
> CXXIII
> Emily Dickinson

Sam the cat checks a cabbage.

IX
ANIMALS OF SERGIEF ISLAND

Probably everyone living in remote parts of the world hopes to be rewarded by frequent sightings of wild animals — in the case of larger ones, at a respectable distance. That rarely happens. In the years we've been here I've seen one bear, and that was after Jeff shot him. True, we see large, clawed footprints padding over the upper garden and down the old road to the used-to-be barn, and large piles of berry-seed-filled bear dung are sometimes scattered near the patches of salmonberry and thimbleberry, but for all the times I go through the berry patches, sometimes with a feeling that sets the hairs along the back of my neck to standing, I've yet to see a bear.

I really don't want to see one by the garden or other close place, but I'd like to see some from the safety of the boat as we go up-river. To prevent seeing one when I'd rather not, I exercise precautions. Each time I'm away from the house area I always announce my presence by banging on my pail or aiming a high-pitched "Home On The Range" aria into the blue with all the power at my command. Bears, I am told, usually yield right-of-way if they hear you coming. Exactly what I'll do if the day ever comes when one doesn't, I haven't quite decided. I've yet to buy the handgun I've always planned to wear in a shoulder holster. I'm not sure I'd remember to use the course of last resort recommended by one book I read: while clasped in the bear's final embrace the victim spits in the bear's gaping jaws. The bear is supposed to find this so disconcerting he'll release you long enough for you to get to the nearest tree. Well!

Bears are one thing, moose another. A moose cow with a small calf came into the cove one summer, climbed the bank, and proceeded to stake her claim. Nobody really wanted to argue with her except Taffy, the miniature dachshund, who kept up such a barking tirade that the moose finally led her little one up into the timber.

Seeing a moose certainly isn't an everyday occurrence, but the animals have looked in the window at me, pruned my young apple trees, swum down and across the river, and paraded their big hoof-prints over the garden. We enjoy seeing them; it makes us know the country is still wild.

Wolves come down the beach occasionally. I hear their lonely call at times, especially when cold closes the land. Once in the dead of winter we looked out a window to see one studying the cabin. The dogs were in the house so there was no one to bark at him. He stood on the frozen river off Chuch Point and seemed to be considering his next action. After about ten minutes he turned and went back up-river.

Often when we stop along the banks of a slough we see the tracks of wolf, bear or moose — animals of the North Country. I'm glad they're there. I want to see them preserved and have no wish to see them driven off the land that is their heritage. Their life is hard. Hunger walks with them along the winter river. Life hunts life along the banks and sloughs of "Stikine River Country."

When man moves into wilderness areas there's always a conflict of interest between wild creatures and the pets and domestic animals with which man surrounds himself. Many of the small creatures — squirrels, weasels, and some of the birds — have disappeared since our arrival. Many times I threaten death to Sam, the cat, when I find birds dead by his fang and paw. Sophie, the Newfoundland dog, considers ground-nesting birds her special prey. Remonstrances and punishment seem to only make her more adept at sneaking her murderous activities.

One creature that's hard to discourage or intimidate is the Sergief Island field mouse. These creatures are not entirely unpleasant except when they're leaving their scat on the cupboard shelves. Tiny, fat-bodied little opportunists, they move en masse into the cabin when the high tides of autumn force them from the flooded marsh flats. I hear their rustling in the boxes stored in the attic; see them poking their heads around the boxes of stored food on the back porch. About then I severely admonish Sam that he's falling down on the job, and reinforce his work with a few judiciously placed traps. The mice are an unsuspecting folk, apparently little affected by community lore, because they often come to the same trap, time after time, without even a change of bait. Their tiny paws reach out to grasp a morsel of food — even after I've left them many a forked carrot in the garden paths to sustain them through the winter.

A tiny white ermine, with a glistening white coat and shiny black-bead eyes, has staked out a claim in the root cellar. He regards us as the interlopers when we enter the room; he sits up on his hind parts the better to observe us. I leave him small offerings of fresh meat that are sometimes accepted, sometimes not. I hope he stays because I've yet to see signs of a mouse in the cellar and the ermine disdains my potatoes and carrots.

When we moved to the island we brought with us a young gray-black Manx cat named Smokey. He was a wonderful fellow, bright and energetic. He'd chase and retrieve a small ball, and loved us unreservedly — more like a dog than a cat. The lady who gave him to us told me he had a small "problem" as she handed him to me wrapped in an old pillowcase. She didn't specify.

It didn't take long to discover what the problem was. He had a genetic defect shared by many of the Manx breed when they have a nonexistent tail; they're unable to control their bladder flow, especially when sleeping.

We took Smokey into the cabin, made him part of the family. When we began to be overwhelmed by the odor of his disability we made special washable beds for him and restricted the places where he could sleep. It didn't help . . . much. Many times I saw him sleeping on a chair, his hindquarters on the edge, a small puddle of urine collecting on the floor.

Much as we treasured him, it became too much to tolerate. The smell of the cabin became distinctive, to say the least. We relegated him to the great outdoors with a bed in the storage shed. Smokey's whole personality changed; he felt betrayed by those to whom he'd given his love and loyalty. He took to wandering farther and farther into the forest around us, sometimes staying for days. One cold winter morning when he'd been missing for several days I heard him cry. Going out to see him as soon as I could, I found he was gone again, leaving nothing but a spot of blood in the snow. We never saw him again until the next year, when we found his shriveled body curled into a storage box where he found shelter after apparently being injured by some animal in the woods.

We miss Smokey still and remember when he and Taffy, the dachshund, played their morning game with a big black raven that made the cove home one winter. Most of the ravens who summer here move to greener pastures when the weather closes us in, probably to Wrangell where they busily raid garbage cans and any container they can rip open with their powerful beaks. Once I found my boxes of groceries torn open, a dozen eggs scattered and other food mutilated, after I'd left the boxes unguarded for a few minutes in the boat while it was tied to the dock in town.

The raven who became familiar to us decided to forgo the pleasures of city life for the winter, but he didn't want to do it without a few subsidies liberally bestowed. Each morning, shortly after dawn, he'd commence his raucous cry. Taffy took his call as an invitation and whined vigorously at the door, ready to meet the challenge. When he saw her coming he hopped from point to point in the cove, staying just far enough ahead of her to give her encouragement. It's my turn now to enter the saga as I go outside to throw away stale bread or pancakes. While the raven slips and slides over the ice to reach his breakfast (he's barely a better ice-walker than I), Smokey makes his move to stalk the bird from the rear. Taffy is barking frantically, her tail a small metronome keeping time to the beat, her hind paws doing their best to claw the ice or snow. She and the raven usually end the morning's performance eyeball to eyeball, until the bird grabs a piece of bread and takes off easily to a giant root on the beach where he eats and laughs in peace.

I don't know what became of him. Never again has a raven become involved with our family, although there are many who come and go over the seasons. Their mating rituals in the early spring are a joy to behold as they perform an aerial ballet, swooping, circling, touching toes, rising in opposite directions to do it again.

As spring sends its irresistible call to the heart of man, bird, and beast, the flow of movement increases over and around the island. Great flocks of ducks and geese call to us from the sky, stopping by the thousand on the marsh flats to feed and refresh themselves before completing their journey to favorite nesting spots on the Arctic tundra. Small birds come in a series of colorful waves, staying for days or weeks depending on available food. Barn swallows come to stay until fall, usually raising their babes in nests under the eaves of porches or the storage shed. They find little trouble filling their crops or those of their young ones when the insects emerge in full force. When I think of how many mosquitoes are consumed by my beautiful blue friends, I'm very thankful for their presence.

This spring again brought my special family of swallows. The past days they've been busily — and vocally — deciding whether or not to once more inhabit the eaves of the front porch. There seems to have been a considerable difference of opinion, but as I write they're settled in, complaining bitterly when I tarry too long on the porch.

Other flocks that please me greatly are the small green wild canaries that relish the elderberries on the big bush outside my kitchen window. Many stacks of dishes have been made light work of as I stood at the sink, dividing the dishwashing with watching them stuff themselves on the bright red berries. Various kinds of birds come to enjoy the bounty of the elderberry, until the last berry has been consumed late in the summer.

Hummingbirds arrive in great numbers in springtime, feeding first off the early fuchsia-colored blossoms of the plentiful salmonberry, then switching their attention to the other berries as they blossom: thimbleberry, blackberry, and currant. They love the fireweed of June and the flowers in my beds, nearly losing themselves in the lovely pink cups of the Canterbury bells. One cat who came to live with us after Smokey died lost her life because of her fanatic expertise at the killing of birds, especially hummingbirds. Even a bell on her neck failed to help; so after picking up two more of the tiny corpses one morning, the death decree was issued.

Sam, the present feline ruler of Sergief, seems to strike a reasonable balance between his hunting instincts and a natural lethargy that makes him prefer to sleep on the rug. He feels a lack in his life, but he's not quite sure what it is. He came here as a small kitten and accepts being one-of-a-kind well until the hormonal juices of spring make him wander. I hear him then, well out into the woods, calling, calling for he knows not what — a lonely Adam in an Eve-less island garden.

* * *

Have you ever watched an eagle walk on solid ground? Plodding awkwardly along, he loses much of his majesty, like an elderly gentleman in need of his cane. Although our "resident" bald eagles are here all year, they are joined each spring by a host of others to feast on the bounty of fish in the river. Often, during the fish runs, I'll see eagles on the beach, holding their catch with one clawed foot while they eat, then walking off with slow deliberation. A far cry from the picture of speed and grace they make in the air.

Close to the beach, down by the old barn road, a tree holds a giant disorderly eagle nest. Most years it contains a young eagle or two. The pair (I don't absolutely know they're always the same pair) make the island their home, and they seem to enjoy watching us going about our chores. Their white heads turn on dark bodies as they mark the progress of my early morning walks along the beach. From "Eagle Tree" they watch for our emergence from the cabin to work in the garden, and they'll stay, overseeing the job, until we go in.

One fall Jeff and I spent a day digging potatoes in the upper garden. All day we heard a recurring cry from the trees near the beach. It was a sad, plaintive wail. When we got close to the end of the job, Jeff, thinking it sounded like some small trapped animal, went to see if he could find what it was. He came back smiling. It was a young eagle who had sat crying all that day; his still-brown head hunched into his shoulder feathers as he mourned the fact of being thrust out into the cold, cruel world. (American bald eagles do not develop their white head and tail feathers until their third year.)

We sight owls, sometimes even the rare pigmy owl; the beautiful marsh hawk; ptarmigan; and the occasional loon, who calls to us as he makes his way up-river to some interior Canadian lake. We're favored by the company of the robber-baron blue jay, robins, and many other species of birds. Aside from the bats who sometimes nest in the attic eaves, the only flying friend left unaccounted for is the gull.

Oh, the gull! When the river comes alive with the melting of the last icebergs and the first run of hooligan starts up the river, the gulls converge by the thousand to feed. For days they cry and swoop; each dive results in the snaring of a hooligan, swallowed so quickly it's possible to miss the process. Thievery is common among them so speed is a requisite. The air is filled with gulls, like white leaves tossed by the wind; the sand bars are obscured by their bodies.

Eagles, too, are there but not in such numbers. The gulls together with the sea lions and seals who also come to feed make spring a time of rejoicing — something to pull you from the nest of bed, fearful of being late for the opening curtain.

Sea lions come with the tide, herds of ten or more, eating, playing, bellowing in true lionish fashion. They sometimes thrust their great bodies of several hundred pounds partly out of the water to look at me or the dogs on the beach.

Each moment of their spring sojourn is treasured by me, shadowed only by the fate of some of the sea lions. They are game to the Native peoples here and I have no quarrel with that. We, too, live off the land. My heartbreak comes when they are killed, driven by high-powered boats up on sand bars with nowhere to go, slaughtered not for food or leather but left to die in their agony as "sport." True, this is illegal, but each spring it happens; each spring another injustice perpetrated upon an animal unable to protect itself against the treachery and technology of man.

* * *

We had expected, by this time, to have several types of domestic animals on the island: a cow or two, or goats, chickens and geese, maybe a turkey or guinea hen or two. None make their habitation here, not even a chick in the spanking brand-new chicken house built so cunningly to house them. A greenhouse on the south side, a root cellar beneath, it's designed to enable each unit to work synergistically with the other to provide heat, food, and fertilizer. Only the root cellar is in use; the greenhouse lacks its glazing, the chicken house its chickens. We fell victim to cost overruns, like our governmental counterparts. Hopefully, time will remedy the situation. I hope to soon see the island a working unit of self-sufficiency.

* * *

No chapter on the animals of Sergief Island would be complete without an account of the life and death of Taffy, the miniature red dachshund who moved here with us as a puppy. She had come into our lives as a gift for Sethnie's eleventh birthday. She was totally lovable; her tiny wrinkled face looked pensive as she scrutinized each one of us and decided to bestow upon us the gift of her love. She never wavered in that decision, and all the days of her life were spent in a dedication of love, rare in the world of humans.

I suppose she really became my dog. I didn't allow it to happen on purpose. She loved us all and slept with Sethnie as long as she was allowed; but between her and me there was a feeling we both recognized, a blending of personalities that developed into a mind-reading affinity. She understood and responded to nearly everything I said to her. I had only to point a finger when she planted her small self on a seedling to cause her to get graciously up and move. Although she dearly loved to go anywhere we did, when we were preparing to go to Wrangell, where we would be staying for a night or two, I left her home because of disease (it's difficult to get booster shots here) and various other reasons. I'd tell her, "Now, Taffy, you'll have to stay home and take care of the place." She'd look downcast but make no move to go out the door as she usually did whenever I went outside. Take care of the place she tried to do, too.

Once during summer I left her outside with Sophie, her big black protector friend. Some boys with motor troubles moored in the cove to try to fix their problem. They later told us the black dog had welcomed their arrival and quickly made friends, but Taffy had never stopped her angry bluster all the hours they were here, challenging them to make a move toward the house.

She dug long tortuous holes in the banks along the river or beside the garden, busying herself in that fashion while I worked in vegetable or rock garden. While I stayed outside, she stayed outside; if I took a nap, she took one too, curled into the crook at the back of my knees.

She was a happy, upbeat little dog, well able to take care of herself under ordinary circumstances. She had no identity crisis or problems with self-esteem; she knew who she was, an important member of the family.

Companion on every walk on the beach or marsh flats, where she had to jump occasionally to see and keep her bearings, she ran along, ears flying out from her head.

She probably can't compare with the genuine heroes of the dog world. She never saved the family from a burning house; she never pulled a child from death by drowning;

but she stood her small ground against anything she conceived as a threat to her family. Her short-legged, fat-rumped little body preceded me up every trail on the island; she looked back occasionally to make sure I was still in tow. At every squirrel tree she stopped delightedly, to bark and dig furiously through the conc duff at the base.

She declared to all creatures great and small that this was her domain — but it wasn't.

One day in July 1984, she and I were alone on the island. Sometimes, when you live in unremitting closeness with other human beings, solitude can be a rare pleasure. We'd come home from town a few days earlier to find the large dog missing; Taffy had been in the house.

This day was beautiful and warm, calling a spirit hungry for summer out into the sun. About noon Taffy and I climbed the path to the strawberry bed, where we ate a few, filled the bowl I'd brought, sat and contemplated the situation for a while, and went back to the cabin. I immediately decided that I needed a head of lettuce, so taking a paring knife with which to cut the lettuce, we headed back.

I have a framed, plastic-covered tomato bed that stands about five feet high. Taffy went up one side of the tomato bed, I the other, so I couldn't see her. As I started through the rows of peas, heading toward the lettuce, I heard Taffy yelp. I've often been warned of eagles snatching small animals, so that was my first thought. I started to run.

I saw no eagle, heard no wings, but I did hear small sounds receding up the trail leading to the upper garden. About halfway up, as I entered a small alder grove, I heard a rustle in the brush to my left and stopped. There a large black wolf stood. When he saw me he lowered his head and brought it back up with Taffy hanging limply from his jaws.

We were about twenty feet apart. Having only my paring knife in my hand, I yelled as loud as I could. For a long minute the wolf and I stared into each other's eyes, then he slowly crossed the trail, taking Taffy with him, leaving only a small puddle of blood in the green plants of summer.

My friend is dead. Gone to feed a creature of the wilderness that I was powerless to stop.

We tried but never caught the wolf. I mourn, wishing I'd done things differently, been more observant, noticed the well-worn trail that led from an upper plateau to near the very edge of the garden; wishing I'd bought and worn a revolver as I've always intended to do.

We're sometimes warned against sentimentally attributing human qualities to animal behavior. Such advice does little for me. Taffy was a loyal, tough little dog. I'll always miss her. One thing cannot be removed, and that is the memory of Taffy and all the animals who have enriched our lives, yours and mine, with their generosity, love and beauty. Simply witnessing the integrity of their lives, be they wild or domestic, gives hope for the ultimate destiny of man.

* * *

There are some tunnel-like holes dug in the bank over the beach. Taffy made each one. Sometimes I'd chide her and tell her she didn't need to overdo it, even though I knew she was a "diggin' dog." She'd be deep in the hole, digging in a whining frenzy for an imaginary quarry, the tip of her furiously wagging tail only sometimes protruding. As long as I'm here the holes will remain, a memorial to one small, red, diggin' dog.

The Sergief Island home is settled in for a Southeast Alaska winter.

X

KEEP YOUR SPIRIT

How do you keep your spirit, maintain good morale in the troops when conditions are trying or unfamiliar?

Probably the most demonstrable help, proved to me, at least, by my own experience, is planned physical exercise. I can see a very real difference in my mental outlook, energy level, and overall good spirits after my twenty-minute regime of stretches, bends and twists every morning. I started this about eighteen months ago, and while it hasn't exactly made me svelte, it has strengthened my stamina, limbered me generally — made me feel better. If the weather is moderate, I do it on the porch or with the door open — all the better to get oxygen — and I move around fast enough to raise my pulse rate. While not a panacea for every problem, it cuts most of them down to size.

Anything that can add cheer and color to your days is of real value, no matter what your situation. It can be as large and exciting as the first great storm of autumn, or as small as sighting the tiny hummingbird of spring.

It must be conceded that one man's tea may be the other fellow's poison: like the rock music that cheers Sethnie and sends her dad up the wall.

Some of the sweetest morale boosters we've received have been the thoughtful remembrances sent us by friends and relatives.

The first winter we were here Lorinda and Bob sent a large box — not Christmas gifts — containing many small, wrapped packages to be opened when we felt we needed a lift. There were books, all the makings for a special fudge, puzzles, games, combs, even a beauty kit (she knows her mother). A marvel of caring creativity.

Doug and his wife, Linnae, sent wood-carving tools and craft kits that were much appreciated.

A gift of love from special friends came in the form of a flurry of letters from nearly every member of one small church. The letters came in on the last mail before freeze-up so they didn't get their answers until spring, but I had all winter to treasure their thoughtfulness.

One friend sent tapes containing all the musical specials at a Bible camp. They were played — still are played — over and over, especially since some of the voices are dear to me.

* * *

The holidays offer reasons to pull out all stops and go for a rousing good time. Every birthday and holiday on the calendar must be taken special note of.

I remember well our first Thanksgiving on Sergief Island. The weather had just notified us of its wintry intentions by a blast of Arctic air. Lloyd had left in September to take care of business in Washington, and it was beginning to look as if he wouldn't be back until spring.

My spirits were low. I was uneasy at the thought of spending the winter alone with the kids in an unfamiliar situation. A bright spot was that Neal, Deveril, and Jacob were here temporarily, working on the cabin they still expected to occupy sometime in the future. They intended to go back to Wrangell in a few days by boat.

The day before Thanksgiving Neal and Jeff went down to the marsh flats to hunt for our dinner. There was a huge flock of snow geese and the boys were lucky enough to bring home a huge one. While they cleaned and plucked the goose, Deveril and I made pies and rolls.

We were used to large family gatherings on all major holidays, and it seemed strange to have so few of us gathered together.

Sethnie loves holidays and did her part to make this one festive: polishing the old oak table and bringing extra leaves down from the attic, making placemats of autumn-toned construction paper, and arranging a red-leafed centerpiece.

The goose was put to cook slowly and tenderly in the oven of the wood stove early Thanksgiving morning. Even Jacob caught the holiday spirit and spent the morning playing, with expectation of good things and practicing the words he was beginning to learn with such interest.

About 2 P.M. we sat down to our first holiday dinner on Sergief Island. Our spirits were good as we looked at each other around the table. After all, we'd made it to Alaska, though the problems were scarcely solved; we were doing what we'd left our homes in Washington to do. We gave thanks to God for His care over us and for allowing us to actually live on an island in Alaska.

When the young couple left a few days later it had to be by helicopter, because ice rapidly building in the river had made a boat crossing impossible. With sadness, I saw them leave in the tiny helicopter — saw the wind catch and toss it as it might a leaf, rapidly carrying it out of my view.

By Christmas we were reconciled to the fact that we (Lee, Jeff, Sethnie, and I) would be alone for the winter. We began to make our plans accordingly.

Since Lee was in Wrangell for the weeks between Thanksgiving and and Christmas, it even seemed doubtful, for a while, if he would be here.

We did our decorating, made cookies — as we've always done before Christmas — and wondered if Lee would get home by helicopter, bringing with him a turkey (the geese had long-since fled the frozen flats).

We made an excursion one clear day to find the best possible tree. Since we're limited to spruce, and many of those are sparsely branched when they grow under larger timber, we settled for one that, though slim, was beautiful. We brought it home through the lengthening shadows of that winter day, the dying sun casting multicolored sparkles over the frozen river — and we laughed. Laughed that we could go out from our cabin and find a wilderness tree; laughed that we were together, crunching along on the crusted snow, going home to a pot of soup simmering on the banked stove. And it was good.

Through the following days we enjoyed an Advent calendar box that contained small gifts for each one as a compartment was opened each night. We weren't without gifts for one another. Secrets were rife, with each one on his honor not to peek in certain places, and the attic preempted many times to give privacy for gift wrapping.

Sethnie cut snowflakes for each small windowpane and popped corn for the tree. It was an old-fashioned Christmas — and we thought we were doing okay.

The only thing lacking was the company of Lloyd and Lee. Lloyd, we knew, we would have to do without, but Lee blew in on the whirlybird just before dark on Christmas Eve. There was a strong wind blowing down-river, so I'd decided he wouldn't be coming, but I looked up at the droning sound of a motor and there he was, the chopper settling softly down on the ice. He came running, bringing the turkey and the other goodies, shielding a lovely little poinsettia that Jeff had sent for. It helped make a great Christmas.

Several other holiday seasons have come and gone since then. Most of them have been spent in much the same way. We try to make much of holidays, preparing for them in advance, stashing treats away in unlikely places. We also make as many of our gifts as possible, and since that's a fun-type job, it's not a burden.

As the population of the island has dwindled (Jeff in college in Idaho, Sethnie boarding in Wrangell to go to high school) it's been harder to keep a luster on the holidays. The price of helicopter transportation has increased steadily the past few years, so accompanied by the other transportation costs involved, the cost to bring the kids home becomes prohibitive. There have been years when it would have been possible to push a boat through the ice, but you could never count on getting out again when necessary.

* * *

Doing things to keep busy and keep your spirits off the ground is important in a situation such as this. Here we are, ice-locked for three to four months a year onto a speck of land where it can take considerable fortitude to bring oneself to leave the cabin. The beach is crusted with multi-layered sheets of ice. It's incredibly beautiful, but doesn't make for pleasant walking; sometimes walking is impossible. The ice-scape changes from day to day depending on the size of the tides that sweep over it. Since the tides vary from twelve feet to nineteen-plus feet, they can make big changes in a short time. Sometimes there are huge icebergs spotting the scene; other times the crusted crystal sheets are picked up by the wind and carried along to be smashed down into cutting shards.

The island trails are usually possible to walk if there's not too deep a layer of soft snow. Sometimes, after a thawing period, the snow refreezes into a slippery sheet that makes walking hazardous. Also, since we haven't been able to make well-kept trails for any distance, most of the way we're fighting through brush. All this is by way of explanation as to why I don't get out much over the winter.

There have been lots of jokes and stories about cabin fever, but in Alaska, as in other northern climates, it can be a very real problem. It must be acknowledged.

In this area our daylight dwindles down to just under seven hours before we're rescued by the always-welcome winter solstice. The daylight hours get progressively less as one moves northward, until you run out of any true daylight at all. This fact undoubtedly contributes to the alcoholism and violence that afflict many cities and villages of Alaska. Even here, nearly eighteen hours of darkness is oppressive. Only by being aware of the danger can precautions be taken.

Keeping busy is a requirement. There's always daily work to do: cooking, washing, necessary cleaning, wood getting and general maintenance. I've found that it's good to have some of those kinds of things that must be done — whether I like them or not. They make me feel I'm justified in spending the balance of my time in ways I enjoy. It also provides a safeguard against depression by forcing me to perform tasks that are necessary to others when I might be inclined to let it all go hang.

Once the weather breaks, the problems diminish; there are vegetables and flowers to plant; the birds and animals have returned; and I'm looking forward to summer plans.

Not that winter doesn't have its special graces. It is the time of year when we get most of our sunny, beautifully clear days. There's a song that says "The bluest skies are in Seattle." I challenge that. The bluest skies are in Alaska. And they come when you think you can't stand another minute of whatever it is you've been complaining about.

So what do you do in a small cabin with five people (now three) to make life interesting? Each of us has his own favorite activity. When Jeff and Sethnie were taking correspondence study, it kept them so busy that any extra time they found never hung heavy. Jeff spent many hours trapping; Sethnie played her piano. Lee is general Mr. Fix-it. He never seems to lack things to do. He also studies and practices amateur radio. Lloyd writes tracts and plays solitaire. I read, write — and rewrite. There are also lots of knitting and crocheting projects, and general sewing. I've actually finished some projects that have been hanging around for years. Crafts interest me, and I have plans for some of the lovely fungi that grow so abundantly on the dead spruce that are scattered through the forest.

Photography is a great hobby. Jeff was my resident expert and I could always count on him to take a well-composed picture. I'm not so sure of myself, but have some lovely slides that would be impossible to replace.

One spring Jeff decided he was going to get some pictures of the eagles nesting with their young on the western boundary of our land, from a nearby tree where he could get high enough to look down into the nest. He made it about fifty feet up into the tree, the eagles watching his every move. After he'd been there a couple of hours the eagles decided they'd been tolerant enough and began to threaten him, so he retired with grace. A full-grown American bald eagle is a large bird with a powerful curved beak, wicked talons and a wing span of six feet or more. The eagles must have looked even larger to Jeff as he kept his balance in that tree. He got some pictures, but even with the telescopic lens they weren't close enough to be good.

Both Jeff and Sethnie have artistic abilities they exercised during their time on the island. They were well supplied with paints, felt-tips and suitable papers. There has been no real lack of things to do — even if one's social life is limited.

I have to admit I've never been a big game player, but we have had some rousing games of Monopoly, pinochle, hearts, and various kinds of word games. We brought lots of games with us and were given more as gifts. They were all used, but if I had it to do over, they'd be used more. Games can be a fine way of sharpening wits and finding a reason to laugh — whether you live in the wilderness or not.

Music — from radio, tapes, and of our own making — has been a big help in keeping us happy. Though our tastes aren't all the same, we make allowances for the other fellow's lack of taste and give each one equal time. (Usually.)

Jeff plays the saxophone, Sethnie the piano. I have an autoharp. I enjoy it and use it, but when I requested it as a Christmas gift a few years ago it was with the idea that I wanted something to sing with. I thought anybody, even I, should be able to play the autoharp. Well, as I said, I play it and enjoy it but there's always the nagging thought that I could be doing it much better. I'd like to listen to an expert.

We have a 12-volt television that adds to our entertainment even though the reception is often poor. We get the Alaskan bush channel and two public broadcasting stations; they provide us with all the television we care for. Use is strictly limited since it pulls down the storage batteries swiftly, necessitating the running of the generator more than we like. The only time the television runs often is during the warmer months when we have to run the generator frequently to keep the freezer going.

The radio is our conveyor of choice for outside information. We carry on lively arguments with talk show hosts, sometimes drowning out the radio speaker and usually wishing vehemently that we could call that turkey and set things straight. News, religious broadcasts and some hours on Canadian radio make up the remaining time.

There's more involved in keeping your spirit in a situation such as ours than getting through the long, dark hours of winter. Isolation in even a balmy tropical climate would pose its problems. It's been a revelation to me to come to understand how much our typical society masks each one of us, our desires and what we do to bring them about. When we're involved with many people, work situations, meetings and entertainments, we often tend to put our own interpretations on the behavior of those close to us, rarely looking too closely at that person. Isolation strips a relationship down to its skeletal foundation; none of the trappings of civilization are left to obscure your vision. It can be chancy, and not easily handled. Anyone anticipating a drastic change in life style that will take them away from accustomed activities, especially when isolation is involved, should be aware that there will be major psychological adjustments to be made.

One necessity is joint goals. If one is convinced what he's doing is for a good and preferably lofty purpose, many trials or inconveniences become minor. If he feels that he's just *putting in his time*, for no reason that he can understand, the reaction is totally different, often with boredom and bitterness.

Money, or the lack of it to do things you consider necessary — and money is essential, even when your goal is self-sufficiency with less dependency on silver and gold — is a problem all its own. I'd be less than candid if I failed to admit that lack of money has stopped us from doing many of the things we planned when we came here, as well as contributing to depression. Frustration is a powerful emotion and you must find ways to circumvent it.

One help, when things look bleak, is to just go and do the thing you'd do if everything was rosy. (That doesn't include a world cruise.) Any work you leave will probably still be there when you return to it, and the string of trout or pail of berries or fungi you bring home will justify your mini-vacation.

Possessions, sometimes small ones, can do a lot to stay a flood of loneliness, bringing memories that allow you to feel — as opposed to mentally knowing — that there are people out there who love you or have loved you. When I use the old rolling pin, missing one handle, that I took out of the small house where my father died, I remember him — his love of animals, the way he played old melodies so expertly on his violin, the beautiful, handcrafted bird-houses he created. I remember helping him, as a small child, to carry in wood, and waiting in delighted anticipation for the chickens to grab the white grubs that fell from the conky wood as he chopped. . . . All this, and more, because I handle one old rolling pin.

When I look up at the large rooster on the wall, made of veneer and given life by the varieties of tacks, staples and nails that indicate its plumage, I remember the many hours of work Doug put in to make it, and all the other contented hours when we worked together on one project or another.

The music box hidden in the body of a tiny sewing machine, playing its plaintive tune of "Yesterday," reminds me of Lorinda and of all the yesterdays we've spent together.

Each item: the woven potholder Lee made in fifth grade, Sethnie's drawing of a Husky dog, the crystal bell Jeff brought us from his Close Up trip to Washington, D.C.; all these things, and many others that form the design on the fabric of a life, are dear to me and precious beyond all relation to value. They symbolize, to me, threads that time and distance cannot break and give me encouragement to carry on.

I swear there have been times since coming here, when my spirits were falling faster than the rain pounding against the windows, that I'd have left on the next available ferry had it not been for the huge old table that graces the main room of the cabin. I look at it, think of its ornate matching chairs stored in the attic, remember the agony of getting it here, think of the improbability of ever removing it, and decide to stay a little longer.

Such is the power of some of the possessions we love.

* * *

Physical health has much to do with emotional well-being, so we try to practice preventive medicine — for that and many other reasons. General well-being is one reason, of course, but another is the near impossibility, at times, of making a speedy exit out of here for medical treatment. Strong winds out of the Stikine basin can last for days, making it impossible for boat, plane or even helicopter to get in.

Keeping up one's appearance is important no matter where you are. As you may have surmised by the recounting of my little economies, I'm no fashion plate. I do, however, try to take care to look as well as possible.

I had babies over a rather longer period of time than most women, so Jeff and Sethnie were born when I might be said to have been over that well-traversed "hill." Since I don't like to imagine they'll remember me as a drab, I give in to small vanities: elastin, moisturizers, anti-oxidents, firm-up, collagen/placenta, cocoa butter, apricot oil. You name it; I've tried it. (I think I've mentioned somewhere in this book that I'm an optimist; and, yes, I know these products aren't supplied by "living off the land.")

I've learned that good looks and vibrant good health depend (barring accident) on proper nutrition, exercise and positive thinking. I don't know if I've converted all my cabin-mates to that line of thinking, but I've convinced myself. Plenty of fruits and vegetables, preferably raw, supplemented by fresh salmon and non-chemical-treated wild meat; outdoor work with a good brisk thirty-minute walk on the beach every possible day; a look at the beauty around me; thanks-giving for the privilege of living in a wilderness wonderland; and I'm set for at least another twenty-four hours.

Jeff, Lloyd, Sethnie, Lee.

XI
SPECIAL THOUGHTS OF SPECIAL ISLANDERS

Jeff raised his head and looked steadily at his dad and me, his quiet voice hesitating as he tried to make us understand how he felt about the island.

"For a long time I felt guilty because I wasn't here. It took awhile to come to terms with the fact that I had to do what seems right for me."

It's the first time Jeff's been home for nearly two years, and he is speaking of the years he's spent at college and the decision he's made for a career that will preclude his ever making the island his home. If his young eyes look troubled they also shine with purpose and resolve that at last he knows it's all right for him to plan a life very different from the one he'd anticipated when he came here.

Lloyd and I never tried to plan the children's lives for them or lock them into life styles not of their choosing. We thought we were offering them something rare in today's world — a chance to make a life in wilderness country. Jeff knows this and his conflict has come not only from what he thought we wanted him to do, but also from his own conflicting desires.

"I really like the island," he says. "I like to think of you guys being here. I'd hate it if you were anywhere else. Living here taught me a lot. I learned how to work and to be responsible for my life. I'm not sorry we came."

It's a joy to me to just sit and look at him after so long. He's a man now, his tall frame more heavily muscled, his words more studied. If I'm sorry he'll never make a life on the river, that sorrow is more than overbalanced by the fact that he seems at peace, and glad about the way his life is going.

* * *

"Which place we've lived do you like the best, Lee?" He gives a grin and the answer comes back promptly. "Oh, I like it best here on Sergief Island. I like Alaska."

Lee is quiet, not given to much talk, so the solitude of the woods suits his personality. If there were one character trait above others I could attribute to Lee it would be faithfulness. If it's a job he can do, he does it — with time-consuming carefulness and no resentment that it may be hard, or one that no one else wants to do.

When the washing machine motor is balky and I've pulled the starter rope until I don't feel up to pulling again, I call Lee. "Could you start this for me?" He checks the oil, perhaps changes the spark plug, and always manages to get it going. He takes on a hundred other projects, it seems. When the hood blows off the chimney; when there's a need for an armload of small, dry wood for a quick fire; when somebody has to crawl under the cabin to staple up insulation; it's usually Lee who goes.

He's small, wiry, and a survivor. I've stopped worrying too much about him when he doesn't get back to the cabin at dark after some trek around the island, because I know the odds are with him. If fortitude and tenacity can make a difference to his situation he'll be okay.

Not that I haven't taken a gun occasionally at nightfall and shot into the air, waiting for a response. From far across the island the answer comes — a lone shot — telling me Lee is on his way home.

"I guess the job I like best is taking the boat up-river to get logs. It's pretty good up there," he says shyly.

I know what he means. It is "pretty good up there." The beautiful Stikine.

* * *

Lloyd sits on his favorite end of the davenport, papers and letters scattered around him. The world comes to him through the mailbox of the Wrangell Post Office — but it isn't the same. He spends weeks and months writing tracts on difficult subjects many religious writers avoid — but it isn't enough. He speaks of his religious and political beliefs with intensity and zeal. A talented public speaker, he's told his views to Lee and me so often the challenge is gone.

It seems that, for him, the idea of setting up a wilderness headquarters was where the fun and purpose were. He never actually expected to get stuck there year-round. Forever? When I laugh and tell him that Moses spent forty years in the wilderness he doesn't think much of my humor. For one thing, he doesn't expect to live to be 120 years old, as Moses did. Time has a way of pressing in on us as we get beyond September.

Lloyd's blue eyes fairly electrify as he explains his position.

"There's a lot going on out there. I can't just sit here."

Maybe not. I've always told him he would have made a great lieutenant to Alexander the Great. He's a mover and shaker and prefers to delegate the petty details of everyday living to more mundane folks, while he concentrates on the big things. When the big things all seem thousands of miles away a problem is posed.

As our opportunities for outside fellowship and stimulation have become more limited the stress of it has increased. It's hardly possible, or even wise, to try to change a gregarious extrovert into a mountain-man loner.

He, too, likes Alaska, appreciates the beauty and majesty of the river. "It's a hard place to top. I just feel I should be doing more and different things than I am."

Sometimes I unclamp my tongue from between my teeth and tell him, "Well, Boyo, there must be a reason for it. It was your idea."

* * *

"It wasn't right for me. When you haven't really proven yourself with other people it's hard. I had to get out of here to find out how to relate."

I understand Sethnie's position. No teenage girl wants to spend most of her life away from all other young people.

We tried to see that she got opportunities for friendships at camp meetings and visits to relatives. Knowing her needs, we'd expected to send her for the last two years of high school to a Christian boarding school.

After a lot of discussion she elected, instead, to enter Wrangell High and live with a family in town. In many ways I'm glad. I can see her often and talk to her daily on the CB. We're not cut off entirely from these years so crucial to any young person. She seems happy, and best of all, from her point of view, she has that thing so essential to a young girl — a best friend, someone to share the jokes, hopes and stings of adolescence.

"I know the island is beautiful, but I'm not a hunter or trapper and I'm not that keen on gardening. I like to have something to get dressed up for sometimes."

Will she ever come back to the island to live? It's doubtful, unless she falls in love one day with a boy who's interested in northern horticulture and the things that are possible here, and has an abiding love for remote living. That might make it all worthwhile to her. Stranger things have happened.

* * *

Neal, Deveril, and Jacob lived on the island for such a short while that it can hardly be said to have had any lasting effect on their lives. The move to Alaska, however, changed their lives dramatically.

I asked them recently if they were glad they'd come. They assured me they were. When they go south each winter to spend the holidays, they tell me they are always anxious to get back to Alaska.

I'm glad they feel that way, since I feel at least partly responsible for them making the move. They're busy, energetic young people, an asset to any state or community. I believe the years they've spent establishing themselves here have brought them closer in their reliance on each other and given them confidence in their own abilities.

* * *

There are other people, scarcely mentioned in this book, whose lives have been touched and altered by our move to Sergief Island. I'm speaking mainly of our daughter, Lorinda, and her family; and our son, Doug, and his family.

Doug has been here once; Lorinda has yet to see the island. This isn't the way I'd envisioned things to be. I have grandchildren growing up who hardly know me. That's a heavy price to pay for remote living, and inflationary at that, as the little ones are added. I keep hoping some of them may turn out to be wilderness people.

The way may yet be opened for at least some of them to live here. Circumstances may make it desirable for them and others to make Sergief Island their home.

In the meantime, I miss them — more than they know.

* * *

Maybe, more than any of the rest, my life has been changed by living on Sergief Island. I know I've become more honest with myself; and I'm sure that except for the long quiet winters I would never have done anything more than consider writing.

Do I love the island more than the others do? It's hard to say. I think I spend more time contemplating its beauty and potential for constructive growth. I think I've grown, for the better, by being here.

I love life; living here has given me some additional small understanding of what life really is. I'd like to share the joy of that understanding with others, here or wherever the Lord may place me. There are some years left; they'll be rich ones.

Each step in writing this book has been painfully, reluctantly taken. I find myself clinging to the first draft, the previous chapter, hesitant to take the next step, fearful of making an irrevocable error.

Then I ask myself, why? There are few really irrevocable errors in this life.

And yet — if I reveal myself, the chinks in the armor of my being that living alone on an island have made apparent, is there a reason for doing so?

Do I have any reason to believe the public would be "enlightened, instructed, or entertained" by reading my book? I don't know. I can only hope that some few might find in my struggles, and the struggles of those others who have lived here, a commonality that might form a bond between us.

Writing so much on one's self is a humbling experience. It's easy to question the wisdom of the whole endeavor. On the other hand, one fears that the reader will find the work egotistical. Who cares what a family does about all the problems — physical, spiritual, and material — they encounter?

So, I "cast my bread upon the waters." May it be food for some out there a bit like me, and all other strange ducks.

Yesterday afternoon we came home on the tide after being in Wrangell for several days. Sometimes in spring we stay a bit longer than usual.

After unpacking groceries and sundry articles, including mail, I found I had several re-usable mailing envelopes, so I went to put them where they're kept. On pulling open the drawer, who should I find but a small brown mouse in considerable agitation. She was unusually brown for a Sergief Island mouse, sleek, and in her way, beautiful.

Instead of darting away, as you would expect a mouse to do, she stood moving her head back and forth from me to a pile of stuffing she'd pulled from a padded mailer. Uncertainty and a sort of pleading seemed expressed in her tiny trade-bead eyes. Undoubtedly she had young ones ensconced in the nest. It was as if she were saying, "Dear God, where and how can I take them to safety?"

I, too, experienced some uncertainty, then I slowly closed the drawer. I'll give her a fighting chance to nurture her brood before having to lead them out into the wide world. After all, I'm a mother too.

Probably that fierce urge to protect my children and grandchildren is one of the strongest forces keeping me here. I want a safe harbor, a quiet spot for them to come — if only for a little while — before going back out into the challenge of the world.

Joy's dressed for a hike in the brush.

XII
WHY ARE WE ON THE ISLAND?

We each came to Sergief Island, mostly unknowingly, for different desires and reasons. Those of us who stay will probably do so for different reasons.

Some things, however, we have in common. We all love the island and appreciate its beauty; we all feel our years here have been years of learning — sometimes more than we'd bargained for; we all feel we've grown emotionally and spiritually by being here. Probably we each know more about ourselves than we did before.

Wilderness tends to make you face yourself — your desires, fears, and true motives. I know that has happened to me. Herman Melville is said to have compared America's concern for the natural wilderness to man's search to understand the wilderness inside himself. I can agree with that.

I know that no matter where Jeff or Sethnie may go, they'll forever carry memories of beautiful Sergief. Jeff won't forget how he and his mother skinned his first bear. Sethnie will sometimes remember the hush over the hollows as we picked berries, with only the bush bumblebees to break the quiet. As we grow older, and an ever-increasing percentage of our life becomes memory, each segment becomes more precious. Memories can never be taken away, so in that sense, Sergief belongs forever to each of us, no matter where circumstance may take us.

Try as we might, we cannot escape the fact that economics forces its heavy hand into the life of each of us. The issue of economics must be faced.

There are various possibilities for bringing in a cash flow. Some are better than others, but they must be suitable to all who would have to be involved. I've thought of a lodge with bed and breakfast. That would be pleasant, would bring interesting people, and since I like to cook would be no great burden, being open only part of the year. It would require, however, a large initial outlay for building so has to be left to the future.

As to the future, there is talk of changing the river. Talk of dams and roads up the mainland side to Canada to facilitate mining and tourism. But then there's been talk for a long time. I hope it stays just talk. I want to see the river running free and wild, and probably in my lifetime that's the way it will remain. But someday changes may happen, so I'm glad I'm here now.

Everybody likes to read a success story — everybody likes to write one. It would be nice to be able to say that everything we'd hoped for and dreamed about had come to pass in the years we've spent here. Or would it?

If things had happened differently, in an easier manner, we'd not have learned many of the things that today are part of our being. All human experience can have value if we learn from it — to use the knowledge in the bettering of the future for ourselves and others.

As I turned back this morning from my walk along the beach I looked beyond a knoll over the river bank. I could see smoke from the cabin rising straight into the air. (There was no wind going into the cove.) At that point, the column of smoke was the only evidence to be seen of man's occupancy of the island. It gave a strange sad tug at my heart. I looked at the steely gray clay banks of the river; at the strong protecting rocks, their various strata interspersed with tiny glistening garnets; at the beach crazy-quilted by footprints of Canadian honkers in the sand; at branches of low-hanging shrubbery flushing red with summer life; and I felt a fierce protective surge of love.

I remember that early spring day when we first landed in the cove. Patches of snow lingered; river dust layered the ground. The abused, misused little cabin looked pathetic. It was dirty, neglected; shotgun blasts had torn through its ceiling; garbage from visiting hunters and fishermen filled every available crevice; a rotting barn, standing in swamp water, gave mute testimony to the death of dreams; abandoned, rusting pieces of old farm machinery still stood where a long-ago owner had left them. But I didn't really see these things.

I saw instead the glory of the river, the beautiful windswept timber lining the shore, the eagle seriously regarding us from the security of the tallest tree, the marvelous rock formations. Most of all, as I knelt to scoop some up in my hands, I saw the sweet soil of Sergief Island, rock-free and rich in humus.

I saw, in my mind, not the scarred little cabin, but a rustic lodge nestled into the rock wall of the cove. I saw, not the overgrown brush-filled plateaus that led away from the cove, but rather, neatly fenced and planted terraces, rich with clovers and other legumes, supporting well-cared-for animals — a small haven in the wilderness with room for several families to live and work together in loving cooperation. It was quite a vision, and like many such visions has yet to prove itself prophetic.

Why should any of it be done? Is there really any good reason for doing those things in this particular place? There are many places with better climates, locations where the obstacles to building a subsistence life style might be more easily climbed. Why choose a spot in a wilderness area with logistical problems, and an annual rainfall of 80-plus inches?

Over the years I've asked myself these questions, and gradually the answers have formed in my mind.

Alaska is a huge state consisting of several distinct climates and topographical areas, none of them offering a gardener's paradise, but along with the problems there exists the promise of great rewards to those willing to search for the key to the treasure. There are, undoubtedly, many in the state who are much more knowledgeable than I about the management of northern climates in respect to gardening; but we are a loose-knit group having little or no communication or exchange between us. I'd like to see that remedied. (I'm not discounting the work done by the Extension Service, and *Alaska Farm and Garden Magazine* in this line.)

We enjoy here probably some of the cleanest waters, the purest air, of any in the United States. There are still few enough people so that we can see another human being approaching with joy and expectation of fellowship. If the climate and the difficulties in transportation have worked toward keeping it that way, we should rejoice. I don't, as the children of Israel did, hanker after the leeks and onions of Egypt; I only seek ways (as minor as possible) with which to modify the wilderness. And I'd like to be involved with a group of people with whom to do it.

Scattered around the bays and inlets of Southeast Alaska are people living in remote spots, some alone but seldom lonely. Some are starting to build lives on homesites they've recently acquired through the state lands disposal programs. These people are here because they, like most of us, long for freedom and independence that can be found here as in few places on earth. Many of these folks possess a wisdom that can be shared.

I'd like to see and know more of Alaska as a whole, and certainly much more about Southeast. This I do know: Aside from the bountiful fish and game we enjoy, nearly every mouthful of food eaten by the folks of Southeast has been shipped here from thousands of miles away. This needn't be so.

While arable land is scarce and hard to come by, there are pockets and scattered spots that could be better utilized, many of them right here on the Stikine. I'd like to see Southeast Alaska more self-sustaining and I'd like to be part of the spearhead working toward that end.

Gold-tolerant varieties of plants are being developed every day; we need to find them. Many people have devoted much of their lives to finding ways to nourish and sustain the soils that give life to our plants and animals; we need to understand and use their findings.

All of us can't move to a remote island, or even own a piece of land in order to produce or procure most of our own food, but we can make a start at cutting the umbilical cord to the supermarket — even if it's simply sprouting a jar of energetic little alfalfa seeds on the drainboard.

We don't need to be chained to the pollutants of pesticides, fertilizers, and chemical wastes that are threatening life in the Lower 48. Here we have, in a sense, another chance. A chance to do it right. Much of Alaska's history has been blotted by those who came, saw, took, and went home, leaving nothing but damage to mark their passing. From the earliest Russian entrepreneur who exploited the Native populations, relentlessly harvesting the fur-bearers to adorn the backs of Russian aristocracy; to gold seekers, only a few of whom stayed to build the state; to the timber barons and fish spoilers, few of whom made their homes or spent their profits here; the story has been one of exploitation. But that has changed. Genuine Alaskans look at their state with appreciative eyes. We don't need to look to other places for the good life — we have it here. Those pioneers who knew all along that this was the spot to be are honored and cherished.

So what has all this to do with Sergief Island? Well, if there's anything this world needs more than food it's cooperation.

Many, probably most, of the people of Third World nations have no land at all. Those with land are finding their little share taken away from them by corrupt governments or multinational corporations, which covet the cheap land as well as the peasant's cheap labor to grow crops for export. Not food to sustain the people who live there, but food and non-essential luxury crops to tempt those who have the dollars to pay, and to help the governments meet the high cost of arms and interest. Surely those of us who possess the possibility of growing our own food should grasp that opportunity with humility and gratitude. We are blessed among peoples, and perhaps we can pass a little of that blessing along.

So, as I thought my long thoughts on my walk this morning I looked about me with rejoicing and gratitude. I'd like to make it possible for others to feel the way I do about this island. This would require commitment and cooperation from everyone involved. There is always a cost. Scripture tells us to count it.

Most of the publications on survival-type living stress only the happy, positive aspects of that way of life. The happy, positive times are there, but folks need to understand there will surely be some negative aspects. It isn't all just heading into the woods with your gun or fishing pole. There will surely be frustrating times and possibly dangerous ones. There will be people who can't, or won't, understand what you're doing in your primitive condition. You'll leave behind much you hold dear. It's imperative that you enjoy and find fulfillment in the works of your hands.

Isolation from the things you are used to is sometimes oppressive; repeated failures in things you try to do require a long suit in patience; the willingness to trade short-term gratification for long-term fulfillment calls for emotional maturity; true cooperation asks that each one has the ability to sometimes say, "You're right. I'm wrong." or "We'll do it again, together."

I don't know what the future holds for any of us here on the island. Perhaps the day will come when some of us regretfully make our way back to more well-worn trails. I hope not. It wouldn't necessarily imply failure, but simply that our wilderness sojourn was over and other doors had been opened before us.

I hope instead that someday the land on Sergief Island will have become a microcosm of what is possible in other northern communities. A small piece of harmony with man and nature, where people can learn and practice the art of growing healthy plants, animals and children in an atmosphere of love.

We nearly all grasp with frantic energy for life. That is as it should be. We're created that way. I don't know why so much of life has to be wasted, whether it's through starvation, disease, or aborted fetuses. Or even more obscenely wasted in the never-ending wars and other methods of self-destruction.

I don't know why. I only know that my God said He came to give us life, and that, more abundantly. I want to play my small part in that process.

The world searches for peace, spends billions of dollars and lives on that search. If it can't be done on one small island in a spot of unutterable beauty and bounty how can it ever be done in the world?

The island has shed its layers of snow for another year, like an old man sluffing the garments of a long winter. The tender flesh of a new summer is showing — new hope in the surging power of life.

> And the work of righteousness shall be peace;
> And the effect of righteousness, quietness and assurance for ever.
> And my people shall dwell in a peaceable habitation,
> And in sure dwellings, and in quiet resting places.
>
> Isaiah 32:17, 18

God bless you all.

RECOMMENDED BOOKS, PERIODICALS AND ORGANIZATIONS

Chapter I

Bromfield, Louis. *The Farm.* Mattituck, N.Y.: Amereon Press, 1976.

Bromfield, Louis. *Malabar Farm.* Mattituck, N.Y.: Amereon Press, 1976.

Alaska Department of Natural Resources
Division of Land and Water Management
Pouch 7-005
Anchorage, AK 99510

Department of Lands, Forests, and Water Resources
Victoria, British Columbia, Canada

Private offerings through newspapers or real estate agencies

Chapter II

Bruyere, Christian. *Country Comforts.* New York: Drake Publishers, 1976.

Kern, Barbara and Ken. *The Owner-Built Homestead.* New York: Charles Scribner, 1977.

Leitch, William C. *Hand-Hewn.* San Francisco, CA: Chronicle Books, 1982.

Rodale Press. *Build It Better Yourself.* Emmaus, PA, 1977.

Rodale Press. *Good-by To The Flush Toilet.* Emmaus, PA, 1977.

Sussman, Art, and Frazier, Richard. *Handmade Hot Water Systems.* Point Arena, CA: Garcia River Press, 1978.

Chapter III

Angier, Bradford. *Field Guide to Edible Wild Plants.* Harrisburg, PA: Stackpole Books, 1974.

Emery, Carla. *Carla Emery's Old Fashioned Recipe Book.* Kendrick, ID: Living Room Mimeographer, 1974.

Fukuoka, Masanov. *The One Straw Revolution.* Emmaus, PA: Rodale Press, 1978.

Furlong, Marjorie, and Pill, Virginia. *Edible? Incredible.* Shelton, WA: Pill Enterprises, 1985.

Patent, Dorothy Hinshaw, and Silderback, Diane D. *Garden Secrets.* Emmaus, PA: Rodale Press, 1982.

Rodale Press. *How To Grow Vegetables and Fruits by the Organic Method.* Emmaus, PA, 1961.

Chapter V

Rodale Press. *Producing Your Own Power.* Emmaus, PA, 1974.

Sullivan, George. *Wind Power For Your Home.* New York: Cornerstone Library, 1978.

Alaska Department of Commerce and Economic Development
Division of Energy and Power Development
3601 "C" St.
Anchorage, AK 99503

Chapter VII

U.S. Coast Guard Auxiliary. *Boating Skills and Seamanship.*

Chapter X

Davis, Adelle. *Let's Get Well.* New York: Harcourt, Brace, and World, 1965.

Gaither, Gloria, and Dobson, Shirley. *Let's Make a Memory.* Waco, TX: World Books, 1983.

Longacre, Doris Janzen. *Living More With Less.* Scottdale, PA: Herald Press, 1980.

Chapter XII

Gish, Art. *Beyond the Rat Race.* Scottdale, PA: Herald Press, 1973.

Lappe, Frances Moore, and Collins, Joseph. *Food First.* Boston, MA: Houghton-Mifflin, 1977.

Various Helpful Information

Alaska Farm and Garden Magazine. Pacific Quest Pub., Anchorage, AK 99510.

Alaska Magazine. Alaska Publishing Properties Inc., Box 99050, Anchorage, AK 99518.

Blair and Ketchum's Country Journal. Box 870, Manchester Center, VT 05255.

Mother Earth Magazine. Hendersonville, NC 28739.

Organic Gardening Magazine. Emmaus, PA 18049.

Publications available through the Library of Congress, Washington, D.C.

People, Food, and Land Foundation
35751 Oak Spring Drive
Tollhouse, CA 93667

Institute For Local Self Reliance
1717 18th Street N.W.
Washington, D.C. 20009
Publication: *Self Reliance*

Regeneration
33 East Minor Street
Emmaus, PA 18049

INDEX